Email the author: tim@ebooksforgolfers.com

Published by:
Bob Thomas Books, Inc.
PO Box 853
Black Mountain, NC 28711

Distributed by:
Bob Thomas Books, Inc.
PO Box 853
Black Mountain, NC 28711

www.ebooksforgolfers.com
www.bobthomasbooks.com

Cover and internals design by Burning Frog prods
www.burningfrog.com

Cover photo by James Johnson
www.fineartofphotography.com

Library of Congress Cataloguing-in-Publication Data
is available upon request.

Printed in the United States of America

Dedication

There is an old adage that behind every successful man there is a woman. That has never been more true than in my case, and I would take this one step further and say that behind every one of my successes a slew of women are responsible. I would like to take this opportunity to dedicate this book to them.

TO JILLI: There is nothing I am prouder of than my decision to marry you. There would be no Director of Golf job, no Master Professional designation, no daring to dream, no book, and no life without you. In short, without you I would not be me as I am right now. Most importantly, there would be no Jackson and there is no way to thank you for that. You are the smartest woman I know and you have taught me more than I can say. Mostly, you have taught me how to love unconditionally. As long as you are the President and CEO of this family I have no worries about our future. Thank you.

TO MOM: Because you were both mother and father, single breadwinner, coach, mediator and the first person to put a golf club in my hand. You taught me that a woman can do anything. Words aren't enough and I can't even try. All I can say is thank you.

TO LORI, KELLY M, KIMMY, JENNY, KELLY B, JODI, JACCI, JILLMA & JESSICA: My one true sister and the ones that adopted me as a brother. Your friendship, laughter and unconditional support have made me a better friend, father and husband. There is no substitute for the sarcasm.

TO AUNT PATTY, AUNT PAT, MRS. REDMILE AND BEAMI: A man can never have too many mothers, especially when they are of your caliber. I have never felt alone knowing you were and are there believing in me.

TO MARY ANNE THOMAS: To say that your belief in this book caught me off guard is an understatement. Knowing that your belief proved my wife right (yet again) is something I have to live with. For your encouragement and the chance, I thank you.

Table of Contents

Acknowledgments

It is virtually impossible to thank all of the people that have helped me on my journey, so if I have left you out, I apologize sincerely. Any omission is unintentional. My memory is feeble.

The following people shall remain with me always. They know why.

Thanks to Jim Cocchi, Murray Conerby, Carl Dukate, Steve Geisler, Jim and Sue Hoy, Jim Johnson, Steve Johnson, Jim Koeniger, Len and Iris Krygowski, Larry Phillips, Ken Scheppele, Harry Shoff, Charlie and Doie Tolbert, Bruce Vittert, Hugh Woltzen and the OWGA (The Oaks Women's Golf Association).

A special thanks to the staff and membership of The Oaks Club—my home for the last 11 years. What I have gained in experience here can never be repaid.

the

FRONT
NINE

A Golf Pro Teaches His Son
About Life & Golf

Tim Beckwith
PGA MASTER PROFESSIONAL

Letter to Jackson

Dear Jackson,

From the moment your mother showed me that little plus sign indicating we were pregnant, my life inexplicably changed. Then the doctor passed your huge, slippery ten-and-a-half pound body into my arms. I know of no way to describe to anyone the feelings that swamp you all at once when you meet your son for the first time. Love is too inadequate a word to encapsulate the flood of emotion that threatens to overwhelm a father nearly every day he spends with his son.

Now, I know your mother will have plenty to say about me making this gender specific, and that I should be more neutral. Almost every time we have discussions about gender, I agree with her completely. It is important that little girls play sports and are praised for their minds, and equally important that boys are praised for their sensitivity and compassion and learn to cook. All children should be supported in learning as much as possible regardless of the child's gender or whether the activity is stereotypically associated with males or females. Yet not all things in life can be neutral, and relationships are one of them. At this point in my life I have a son—you, my favorite boy. If your mother ever gifts me with a daughter, I will cross that relationship bridge when I get there.

People say, "Oh, you know how fathers and sons can be" for valid reasons. I have made it a personal goal not to fall into the trap of competition and one-upmanship that can color what should be the beautiful experience of being a father and being a son.

Perhaps I am so sensitive to this because my father was not readily available to me. The reasons for this matter little. I found myself blessed instead with a very strong single mother of three, your Grandma Cookie, who taught me to respect women immensely. My mom. The first person to put a club in my hand. Tough, fair, extremely funny. She wouldn't put up with a lot of bull from us kids. She is one of the hardest workers I know.

And further, I was granted three amazing father figures: your Grandpa Jack (yes, we named you after him), your great-uncle Rod, and your mother's father, Grampie. I wish you could have met the first two. You are fortunate to know the third.

Grandpa Jack. My mother's husband and the father of my heart. He and my mom didn't marry until I was thirteen, but he was what I believe a dad should be. He was completely unselfish, a soft touch, protective and fair.

Uncle Rod. My parents divorced when I was only one. Uncle Rod was unable to have kids of his own and adopted all of us (my cousins, sister, brother and me) as his own. My summers were full of family because of him. (I speak of him at length in the Perspective chapter.)

Grampie. A completely self-made man. He came from a poor family that didn't have the first clue about nurturing. Probably next to your mom he is the smartest person I know. Grampie graduated from high school when he was sixteen, then had his own business by age eighteen. He believes in Christmas and family. Grampie has embraced me as one of his own and made me a part of an incredible family.

These men taught me a great many things. None of them were perfect. One didn't always prioritize correctly, one didn't always hear me, and one didn't always "get" me. But they all tried. That is the lesson I have learned as a father: Try.

Perhaps I should give you a little background before I explain the reason for this book. You see, Jax, you were not our first attempt at making a baby. Although we went through several years filled with heartache, your mother and I believe it took all of that to make you: our perfect son. We believe it made us appreciate you, value you, and treasure you more than if we had been able to make you our first time out. One of the tenets of my life has been that working harder for something makes you appreciate it more. That has never been truer than it is in regards to you. For the gift of you, I thank your mother and God every day. I believe that I should return the favor to you. This book is what I can humbly offer to my favorite person.

So perhaps now you may have a slight understanding of what this book means to me. From the moment I met you, I have believed that my job, my duty, and my pleasure in life is to help you on your journey in any way I can. This is not an ego trip. I don't wish to mold you into a better version of myself. You were born better than me. To understand that last statement, you would have to be a father. (God, I hope I get to see that!) Your mother is in you and that is a very good thing. I only hope I can be what you need me to be.

I don't believe that drilling instructions for life into your head will make you a better man. From my experience, I believe that would only serve to cause resentment. I am not going to pretend that you will learn everything you need to know from my blunders or lessons. You will make your own mistakes, and you should. And please don't use this as a bible. I am not here to preach, but to offer. This writing is for you to use as a guide if you ever have any questions and I am not around to answer them, as a "when in doubt, consult the book" type of thing. My feelings are fairly clear on these subjects, so it should be an easy read. Use this gift as you will.

I do know several things however, and I want to share these with you:

- I have more life experience than you. (This will change in due time, believe me.)
- I have probably spent more time on a golf course than off up to this point in time.
- The lessons I have learned on the links apply as much on them as off.

Most importantly, I know this: I love three things more than anything in the world—you, your mother, and the purity that is the game of golf. This sharing of the lessons I have learned from the game that I love, the game that puts food on our table, the game that is a constant learning tool, with you, my son, is the greatest joy I could have next to having you in my life.

Love, Dad

Play Fair

I have seen several examples of cheating in my time, and they always serve to put a knot in my stomach and rage in my eye. A particularly disappointing version that seems too acceptable in my way of thinking is the padding of handicaps. A *handicap* is a mathematical measure of an amateur golfer's playing ability based on what tees are played, the course and the number of holes played. The lower the handicap is, the better the player. This allows amateur golfers of all levels to play together somewhat as equals. When someone pads his handicap he is making that handicap number higher to present himself to the other golfers as a worse player than he actually is. How this helps the person cheat is that during tournament play the player will have that higher handicap, play at a better level than that handicap and still get that handicap stroke reduction, thereby lowering his score even further than if he had played on his real ability.

I know why people do it. I've just never understood the idea behind it. The concept of making yourself sound less capable than you are isn't just unfair. It's deceitful. Those are strong words, I realize, but let's give the devil his fifteen minutes. Dishonesty is out there; you just don't have to participate in it. I certainly hope *you* don't.

While I would love to spout off about my inability to cheat and what a great guy I am, it would only serve to make me look like an ass. In general, I would rather not *ever* look like one, especially in front of you. So, because the real lesson here is about honesty, I will not lie to you. Ever.

My deepest shame, my son, is that I have cheated. At these times in my life, the lesser version of me won out over the better person I should have been. The very cornerstone of my coaching as a pro is the necessity for the student to be able to self-teach. This skill involves having enough pride to be honest with yourself as you embark on a task. I will use the driving range to illustrate. When a student tells me he hit 240 balls, he wants me to be impressed. Believe me, I am, most of the time. Physically, that is a daunting task. Psychologically, it can be numbing. When I ask him what he taught himself during the exercise, the blank stare I get in return is less impressive.

The golf course can be a lonely place. The same can be said for the driving range. There are only you, your clubs, and the ball. A perfect trinity, if you choose to embrace the most important aspect of the triangle: you. Your mind should never shut down or equivocate. Your mind should be looking for ways to improve constantly. While perfection is never attainable and, in my opinion, should never be sought (more on this later), the more you self-teach the less you deceive yourself. Having enough honesty about and pride in both yourself and your chosen endeavor is the greatest version of playing fair. To hit 240 balls with no conscious thought is doing yourself an injustice—you aren't trying, you aren't learning. Denying yourself the chance to work toward the whole experience (no matter what your task) is both lazy and wrong. I'll grant you that it isn't the traditional definition of cheating, but to me it's just as important. I hope that I am much more aware now as a teacher than I was when *I* used to hit hundreds of balls with no thought! Let me elaborate on why both kinds of dishonesty aren't worth it.

My first foray into the "dark side" of cheating wasn't on the golf course. I was a freshman at Springstead High School. This confession may shock you. Yup, it doesn't get any more stupid than this. A "friend" gave me the answers to a multiple choice quiz in Spanish class, and I memorized them (B,D,A,C,A,C,B,C,D,C,F,F,F,T,T,F,F,F,T,T). So while I know a list of letters by heart and passed the test, I still cannot talk directly to ten percent of the population of this country, a regret I live with daily. Son, I should know how to speak Spanish. If I did, I would be more well-rounded and a better asset to my bosses. This is an excellent example of being unfaithful to yourself in the purest form. If you can, master a language that isn't your native tongue. The ability to learn anything is as important as the knowledge you store in the end. Unless you lose your mind, neither can be taken away from you. You will be better for it.

Now, the second way of cheating is doing it to beat someone else. This is unquestionably low. Not only have you denied yourself the full experience of victory, but you stole someone else's triumph on top of it. Some people do this without a qualm and never lose a night's sleep over it.

Believe me, I have seen it. I have to think these people have no conscience, a situation that your old man is not familiar with at all.

The second time I cheated, my behavior was so reprehensible that I still cringe while I write this, even though it happened twenty-four years ago. Yes, it's that bad. The sinking feeling, the loss of integrity, the feeling that I'll never crawl out of the hole I dug for myself. I had those feelings then, I have them now.

During my freshman golf season at the before-mentioned Springstead High, I was fortunate enough to have earned my way into one of our district matches. I thought, for a moment, that I was hot stuff. Then self-doubt reared its ugly head.

If there is one thing I would like to get across to you more than any other lesson, it would be that you are your own power. Your mind can control only one thing in this world (unless you end up having some superpower of which I am as yet unaware). That one thing your mind controls is you. This includes your responses to outside forces, people, and situations.

So, as you may guess, my mind's reaction to participating in this particular tournament wasn't stellar, to say the least. I was nervous. I was doubtful. I was outwardly arrogant and inwardly terrified. In short, I behaved like a little twerp. I was only a freshman, but I must have been somewhat good, because I was getting to play the older kids. This was a big freakin' deal. At least it was to me—and your grandmother, of course. But I digress. On the day of the tournament, I stunk. I was just awful. There isn't any other way to say it. The remarkable thing was that I didn't realize that things could get worse.

On a certain par five, your dad hit his tee shot into the palmettos. Now my opponent, a junior who was keeping my score, hit his in the fairway (of course). This left me to my own devices in the brush. Jax, I hacked and I whacked at that damn ball until I finally popped it out. By the time I reached the green and tapped in my final stroke, I made nine. To this day, my biggest shame is telling that junior that I made an eight.

Go ahead, you can laugh. People have, and will continue to whenever they hear this confession. It doesn't seem like a big deal when you're already in last place in the tournament. But I also put myself in that rank as a human that day, and that is my regret.

I can also tell you that I had fourteen holes left to win that tournament, or at least to come back a little in order to place. Yet after I lied, I was wrecked. I couldn't concentrate. I felt like I was going to be disqualified at any minute for cheating—the worst offense that one can commit, in sports and in life. The sweat trickled down my back, fear pricked my mind, and the shame broke me.

A bad day of golf yielded a valuable lesson I would apply both on and off the course. I realized that win or lose, I would rather play a game my way—with integrity. This was the only way I could play golf and still get to sleep at night.

As a P.S., I would like to say something to you about a different kind of deception altogether, as I feel *very* strongly about it. Please don't fool around on your significant other. Breaking promises and vows just isn't right. Know yourself well enough not to make a promise in the first place if you can't stay faithful and loyal. If you are unfaithful to your partner, you degrade the entire relationship. You deny yourself the experience of knowing the fulfillment of giving *one* other person everything you have. In addition, if you have children, you have not only cheated on their mother, but also on them. You can't do this and have your children's highest interests at heart. In my opinion, it just isn't possible. They deserve a full-time father who keeps his eyes on the family and makes them his main priority. If you make a promise, keep it. Try.

*The most important rule in playing good golf is to understand your ultimate goal: shooting the lowest possible score. Sounds easy, right? The way to achieve this goal is to be steady. I have said to students for years that "the only way to **be** consistent is to **think** consistently." I mean that you are able to perform the same shot or have the same mindset repeatedly. In order to have the same outcome on a shot every time, your setup, posture, ball position and certainly your swing thought need to be the same.*

*To practice "one thought" is to have a mantra you use, in this case, during the golf swing. The swing is so short in time (1.27 seconds on average) that focusing on more than one thing is nearly impossible. The "one thought" certainly could be different from one person to the next. Perhaps the most common thought on tour is: **Tempo**. I have some students who only swing with their arms and don't turn their body. In this instance, most of the time I suggest the thought: **Turn the sternum** (the breastbone). After they get in the habit of turning the sternum, the thought may change to something else that would be determined by a professional. Whatever the thought is, it is imperative that it be positive. The mind does not register negatives well.*

This "one thought" will change with context, but remember: you must practice this technique **over and over**. It is the only way to achieve true confidence on the course. This may sound boring, but no one said becoming great at something was easy. If it were, we all would do it! Many students do something differently on a subsequent shot, simply because the shot before wasn't very good. You must continue to set up with the body in the same position each time and have the same "one thought" with each swing; this is how you hit consistent shots. You must remember that if it works during practice, it will work during a round, as long as you trust it. Many players hit balls on the range without thinking, then get to the first tee and cannot perform. Why? They think differently now that there is a consequence. Well Jax, don't worry about the consequence; worry about what you are thinking and you will be just fine!

"One thought" in the real world is also essential because I don't believe in multi-tasking on the course or in life. I believe in complete focus on one task or challenge at a time. I believe this makes me more efficient as a player and a person. This strategy may not work for everyone, but it works for me.

Do Unto Others

Do unto others as you would have them do unto you. It is called the "Golden Rule" for a reason. And while I hope not to be trite or repetitious during your childhood (God knows I would hate to be boring!) this one bears repeating.

You will find that most of these nine lessons are in some way a variation on this theme. Indeed, perhaps this chapter should have come first, as this concept should pervade every moment of your life. But I stand by the order I've put them in, because playing fair begins within, and this rule requires outward action. You cannot treat others well if you don't start with yourself.

So that brings us here, to the next in my

progression of life lessons. It's my logic and my book, so just go with it, even if you don't get it at first...

When I was a young boy, I was what you would call a smart ass. I should admit now that I have yet to outgrow that certain aspect of my personality. It isn't a particularly heinous crime against humanity. As a matter of fact, according to your mother, it was one of the reasons she fell for me. I made her laugh. Her standards are extremely high, so I trust her judgment on this.

We will explore the importance of an excellent sense of humor more throughout your life. For now, however, I must confess that your father doesn't always know when to quit or when he isn't that funny.

I could certainly regale you with story after story of harmless fun amongst boys. Pulling out chairs from under comrades in arms during spelling class comes to the mind rather quickly. While these types of discretions are by no means nice, an innocence permeates them because of one thing: We didn't know any better at the time.

As I am writing this to you with the hope of you getting some value from it, I will dig deeper and force myself to offer another uncomfortable confession.

Let me begin by speaking for a minute about boys in middle school. I feel confident in writing on this topic, having had firsthand experience for three years. Something happens to boys in the sixth grade. I am not sure exactly what it is, but I have my theories. One of these is that all of a sudden the realization occurs that the inevitable conclusion to their childhood is adulthood, with specific emphasis on "becoming a man." It doesn't help that the men around them start to treat them differently—as if their feelings, hurts, or sensitivities should no longer be nurtured, and that now, having reached double-digit ages, they should become less sensitive or even (God forbid I utter this) less sweet.

Yes, Jax, you were sweet. As I write this, you still are. I hope you will always be my good-natured boy, with your toothy smile and big hugs for daddy. Yet my feelings are bittersweet as I write this, because I know it's almost inevitable that the men and boys around you will become so intent on making sure you're "a man" along with them that you might lose that innocence. It will most likely happen by your own doing as well. Sixth-, seventh-, and eighth-grade boys have a powerful need for acceptance. A need to make a mark or stand out among peers almost guarantees that most boys of that age will apply for membership into the "man club."

You can make your mark, of course, by doing any number of things. Not all of these are necessarily bad. You could be genuinely smart, or athletic or funny. You could even be really good-looking or a great singer like your mom, but my advice is not to let any one thing define you.

Of course, in my humble opinion a ticket to the "man club" is highly overrated, especially if your entry begins with hurting someone else, either physically or emotionally. Jax, the character traits of a "man's man" that I grew up with are name-calling, putting down others, and over-zealous competition, with not enough emphasis on brains and too much on brawn. I don't need you to be this kind of person and hope you don't either. I hope you are not afraid to be sensitive to other's feelings. I hope you don't strive to fit in with "the guys" if what they are doing disagrees with your core values.

Where I grew up boys couldn't like pink. If they cried they were wimps. These limits grow into a culture of their own by the time a boy gets to his teen years in that he is afraid to show any emotion other than what is socially acceptable. Fear, sensitivity, compassion and kindness garner derision in that world, but screaming because of a bad shot is considered okay. I am not okay with that. I hope to get across to you that I would like to see you focus less on this culture's ideas of what it is to be a man and more on the traits of being a good person.

I wish fervently that I could spare you the uncertainty of these years, even though I know I can't. My hope is that by learning about my experiences you will make better choices than I did. Since I have stalled long enough in confessing this particular sin, I will jump right in.

When I was in eighth grade, I had a teacher who was a little, shall I say, boring. He was to me, anyway. Unfortunately, at that time in my life I didn't get that listening to other people who had more knowledge than I did was a good idea. I was one of those jokers who thought he knew everything. I had also defined myself among my peers as a "class clown." This distinction isn't a bad one. It's just that I allowed it to become my main job in school. Uh, yeah, over and above cracking the books. Again, I could make this a lesson about studying hard and focusing; those things are vitally important. I am *way* more interested in your becoming a good person than someone who is intelligent yet also a jackass.

During this class I found various ways of ignoring the teacher, who was soft-spoken and shy and read straight from his notes. The kids thought I was hilarious. Finally, I came up with the ultimate way of showing the instructor who truly ran the class.

Each day, as he would begin the lecture, I pulled out the newspaper. I read the sports page to the class every single day. And every single day, the teacher kicked me out. I had to wait outside the door until class was over. Looking back, I realize that he could have sent me to the office for this offense and I would have had a referral on my record or I would have received a paddling (yeah, they spanked back then). Obviously, he was far more decent than I was.

I share this with you now, because what I did was extremely disrespectful and positively not funny. It was actually plain stupid. (I mean, I missed out on gaining almost an entire year of knowledge.)

The bigger offense here was that even though I knew it wasn't nice, I did it anyway. Even though I knew I would *hate* for someone to do it to me, I did it anyway, just to get a laugh. Actually, writing it down now, it seems even more unforgivable. It is also kind of ironic, since I ended up being a teacher.

It's almost a definite that I hurt that teacher's feelings. For what? To impress some kids, most of whom I never saw or talked to again after the age of eighteen. It wasn't worth it.

See, because of this experience, I believe that practicing the Golden Rule isn't about being nice to others so they'll be nice to you. For me, it's about treating others well, so I don't feel like garbage.

When bringing this lesson to the course, I have to explain something I haven't mentioned yet: *psychological warfare*.

Almost every man who calls himself an athlete will tell you that getting into someone's head during competition is part of the game. I know several women who do it as well. In my experience, however, it's more prevalent among men. My theory is that women have a tendency to turn the competition inward. Whether they are playing a sport or tackling a life challenge, their approach is more about their own focus than their opponent's failures. They also seem to blame themselves incessantly. With men, it's about getting the edge.

I am not going to sit here and tell you not to do it or that I haven't done it; I have, too many times to count, as a matter of fact, when I was playing for money or status. Hell, one of the reasons your mother took two weeks to go out with me a second time was because she found out I went after your Uncle Joe's mind in an effort to win some cash off him in a skins game. She asked me why I was playing golf in the first place if I wasn't good enough to win based on my own skill. She asked if it felt like a hollow victory when I won that way. It hadn't, until she put it that way. Bright woman, your mother.

I will tell you that it's a fine line you walk when you go after someone's confidence. There are two lessons here. Not only do you have to make the personal decision as to whether you are going to play the game this way (and by "game" I mean any sport you choose, any endeavor, job, or life's work). In addition, you have to decide how you will react when someone goes after you in a similar manner.

The paradox of the golden rule in sports is: If you dish it out, be prepared to swallow some of it as well.

Now, I'm not going to promise you that if you're Mr. Nice Guy, people won't attempt to mess with your head. My only concern is you and how well you sleep at night. Your only gauge on how to handle a situation correctly is to ask one question:

How would I feel if it were me? The answer will guide you in the right direction.

*Putting is the key to good golf. It is not sexy nor is it going to show how big and strong and long you are, but it is what turns a good golfer into a champion. This is the portion of the game that separates the winners from the also-rans. Before you were born, I created a concept called "Four-Foot Confidence." It is simple, and some may say stupidly naïve, but anything that leads to more belief in oneself on the course works for me. Four-Foot Confidence is based on the idea that if you **believe** you can make all ("most" is beyond exceptional and damn near impossible) putts from four feet and in, you will make the rest of the game much easier; each shot prior will be less stressful and thus give you a greater likelihood of success. Golf is a game that builds on itself. If you master what most would consider a mundane shot, your confidence (and then your ability) grows exponentially.*

At this point, you're probably asking yourself, "What do I need to do to putt well?" Just as with every shot in golf, the route to success lies in the setup, and in putting there is one key that I will share with you as well.

Before I do so, I will cover your setup. To begin, examine your posture; make sure your spine is nice and straight. You're lucky on this one because you have your mother's natural posture, but you just need to make sure you have your tailbone sticking out. *(Yes, it feels weird and you'll think you look weird, but I assure you, it isn't and you won't.)* The next step is to make sure your feet, shoulders, and hips are all parallel to the **target line**—*the line you want the putt to start on, not always the one straight to the hole.*

Not knowing whether you are right- or left-handed, I will default to the right hand for this particular lesson. When you are putting right-handed, the position of your left hand and left palm are most important. *(If you are putting left-handed, the opposite is true.)* Now, you need to take your grip and make sure the back of your left hand is facing the target and your palms are facing one another.

Most people want to putt with their wrists; you and all good putters, however, will keep your wrists very steady. To do so, focus on the amount of pressure your left palm has against the putter grip. Make sure it remains the same at all times. This will ensure the putter face is square to the target line at all times. Good luck.

One-Hundred Percent

Well, Jax, this is a tough one. Because although it sounds simple—give one-hundred percent in everything—it actually involves downright hard work and most of the time some even tougher choices.

It's a hell of a lot of pressure to put on you, especially given the fact that while I am writing this chapter, you aren't yet two years old. What I would like is if you could make it a long-term goal, knowing that you won't always meet it, but that it's there in the distance and achievable.

Back to those choices again, and how challenging they can be. When I was a young man of nineteen, I drove two hours daily (one hour each way) to get to college. Living at home was much cheaper. We didn't have a lot of money. I was on a scholarship for golf and more than anything in the world, I wanted to be a golf pro. I mean, the real deal. An actual touring professional. This was not out of the realm of possibility. I was good, if I do say so myself. There was raw talent, tremendous drive, and a big-time desire to prove myself. My coaches agreed, and I continued the commute to school every day.

Then. I. Met. A. Girl.

These five words belong in a class of their own. I'll strive to help you navigate that mysterious feminine path as much as I can when you cross it, but I am no expert. That ought to be obvious, given the fact that it took me until the age of nineteen before I actually got a girlfriend. I was a late bloomer. At the time, I bemoaned this fact. Now, I am quite pleased with how it all worked out. But that is not the point of this book. We'll discuss it at length when you're thirteen.

She was perfect. She was the one. Or so I thought. She truly was a good girl. Or a "nice girl," as we put it back in the day. She came from a good family and had a good head on her shoulders. (Your father has a soft spot for brainy women.)

We grew serious. Several years went by. I made

decisions: to quit school, to pursue golf another way, to move, to work at a cart barn and to play golf for money. Not once during this time did I give any of these choices one-hundred percent of my focus. So I failed at all of them.

Then I asked the girl of my dreams to marry me. I asked her father for his blessing. Though he didn't want to give it, he did so begrudgingly, but not before asking how I intended to take care of his little girl. I will pause now and say that this response was extremely old-fashioned and a little sexist, especially given the fact that his little girl was now a nurse and was making more money than I was. That doesn't mean I don't understand why he asked. He inferred that I was playing at life and I needed to find a path. Whether I liked him or not, he was right.

Putting our heads together, my fiancée and I decided that I should quit pursuing golf and join a local accounting firm. Shocking, but in my defense, I am pretty good with numbers.

I took accounting classes and honestly tried. It was for her, after all, and I loved her and wanted her to be happy. She didn't understand how any normal person could find any real job security in golf, and it didn't look like I was going to make it on tour anytime soon, so I tried. I made it a year and a half.

The work itself was fine. It came easy to me and I cruised along, heading for CPA prison. At least that's what it felt like to me, a guy who so loves golf. I told my dream girl I was miserable, and she agreed I should try a golf job again.

We lasted only a little while longer. I want to say that none of this was her fault. She was a sweet girl. In the end though we didn't understand each other's desires. She needed security and stability and I had to realize my dream. Those two paths were opposed. We parted ways amicably.

My point here is this: If I had been willing to give one-hundred percent to any of my choices during that time period, things still would *not* have worked out. Of course, I can say unequiv- ocally that I am happy my life went the way it did, for several reasons. The biggest of them all is you.

What I truly believe is that if your pursuits are meant to be, giving wholly to them won't be such a struggle or a trial. It will still be damn hard work, but you will want to give that much to them. I couldn't give myself heart and soul to her or what she needed, and she couldn't change for me. Tough choices had to be made. Anyone who doesn't understand you and what makes you tick will not be the one.

Case in point: A year later, at the ripe age of twenty-six, I was working in golf again and was having some success. I still believed I was going to find a sponsor who would take me away from everything so I could just practice all day and win tournaments, that I'd have no work to worry about and would reap all the benefits of another's benevolence. This was how I believed I was going to make it on tour.

Then. I. Met. A. Woman.

Whoa boy, buddy. This was it. She was the one, and good Lord, did she kick my ass. I don't mean that in a bad way. I mean that she had high standards, and I wanted to meet them. She didn't test me or anything, but she caused me to want to challenge myself.

This was a relationship. The future was contemplated. Dreams were shared, and it became clear that choices (again) had to be made.

Your mother (I imagine you guessed this woman was your mother) believes in dreams. Pursuing them, working toward them, and ultimately succeeding in making them a reality. She believed in them when we met. I began to believe that with her by my side, anything was possible.

We share the common threads of being deeply

rooted in family, having had an exceptional talent that helped guide us through our young lives, and having suffered through crises of confidence because of said ability.

This was an excellent foundation to build on, but first we had to decide on our goals. Your mother knew before I did that I would not be happy unless golf was part of my daily life. She followed me around the golf course for qualifiers more times than I can count. She pushed me and believed in me. She gave me one-hundred percent. I'd like to think I gave the same in return, but I know that wasn't always the case. We did move to Nashville so she could pursue a singing career. She pushed me so hard during that time that I was able to finally become a Class A PGA professional.

You see, while your mother believes in dreams, she is also a very practical woman. Since I wasn't winning any of those qualifiers, it was realistic to see if I could achieve the highest level of education possible in my chosen profession.

Your mom knew before I did that another choice would have to be made. So if I wasn't good enough to play golf on tour, I could still be around the game every day and be fulfilled by helping others achieve their potential on the course.

The ultimate choice came for us both after

several years together. It was, as your Grampie likes to say, a "shit or get off the pot" moment. Your grandfather likes to cut through to the heart of a situation.

Anyway, we had been together so long (almost six years), that we had to decide what came next. We were both working toward separate dreams and neither was coming true in the ways we imagined. We had tried to support each other in these endeavors. Then we realized that we would need to focus on one thing at a time. We had always agreed that we didn't want kids unless one of us could be home with them. (Both our moms had worked hard during our childhoods and we wanted something different.) That was one of the major reasons we hadn't gotten serious about getting married. Yet the time had come. We tried being apart first to see if we could live without each other. Needless to say, neither one of us could give ourselves heart and soul to that effort. Your mom and I are meant to be, kid.

So, because your mother is an outstanding partner and, if possible, an even better motivator, I was able to achieve a high level of success in my career during this time. Your mother's choice was tougher. She chose to give me one-hundred percent of her so I could give myself wholly to my career and we could both give our all to you.

These were not hard choices, because we got you. Like I said before, if your path is meant to be, giving it everything you have will seem right and natural, like a given. I'm not saying that it doesn't take effort to get up every morning and work at it, but there is pure joy at the end of the pursuit. That's how you know you're giving wholly of yourself to the right person, path, sport, or career—by the joy you still feel after the work is over.

In relating this lesson to the golf course, the importance of practice leaps to my mind immediately. Most of my students do not love the driving range, as there is no competition, no score, and sometimes no finite success. Some students do not love the course or applying the knowledge they learned at the range to actual play. Both routines are necessary. Both require one-hundred percent commitment and hard work. If the game of golf is your passion, your pursuit, and your path, then the joy you get in return compensates for anything else. Later I'll say more about my theory of practice. (See Chapter 5.)

While on the course itself it is important you give your all to the effort. You might play alone or in a *better ball event* where a partner is counting on you. (A better ball event is when two players are on a team and they can choose the better score of the two on each hole.) If you are not totally focused, you don't belong on the course that day. I am not saying not to enjoy yourself. You can have fun and give your full attention to the game, too. A pet peeve of mine is slow play which I see as the epitome of not giving wholly to the effort. If your sluggish ways (when you are fully capable) constantly cause players in your group or behind you to have to wait for you, not only is your behavior rude, but it also shows a lack of attention on the whole experience of being on the course. Again, if you can't give one-hundred percent, even if the round is just a couple of folks golfing for a good time, then play another day. You don't belong there.

LESSON 3

I began with putting. I'll now tell you a bit about **chipping.** *Putting and chipping are alike in that they are the two shots that only utilize one lever: the shoulders. (Understand that the shoulders are one of two levers that are used in golf at any time. The other is the wrists.) In both shots you do not use your wrists.*

The differences between these shots are in the club that is used, as well as the positions of the body and the ball. In putting, you use your putter, and in chipping, you can use a sand wedge, pitching wedge or any short-iron (seven, eight or nine). There are two differences in the body position. The first is that the stance is square to the target line when putting, and open (the feet are aimed left of the target line if you end up playing right-handed) when chipping. The second is that the weight is evenly distributed on each foot while putting but slightly on the forward foot when chipping (approximately sixty percent on the left foot for right-handed players). In putting, the ball is in the middle of the stance or slightly forward from center. In chipping, the ball goes to the back of the stance.

There are a couple of things to keep in mind when chipping. One is to keep the ball as low as possible and another is to land the ball on the green whenever possible. These may contradict each other in a way, but see if you can understand the thinking. Keep the ball low because the lower you hit it, the less of a swing is necessary; thus you can have better control and more consistency (there's that word again). Land the ball on the green because you know more about what to expect when the ball lands on the green versus when it lands on the fringe, fairway, or rough: **the longer the grass, the greater the unknown.**

Now that you know all the positions, there is one thing that I want to point out regarding the "no wrists" thing. When chipping, the wrists should not break or hinge, as doing so causes the clubhead to go higher in the air than it should. Concentrating on keeping the clubhead low to the ground generally forces you to keep your wrists quiet. Your attention can then be on the clubhead rather than the wrists. Keeping the clubhead low to the ground on the way back and through also gives you the most consistent roll of the ball when it hits the green.

If you perfect these two short, simple shots—putting and chipping—(perfection is not possible in golf, but you can get close), you can shoot **even par** regardless of the other factors in your game. You should spend about seventy percent of your practice time on these two shots. (**Par** for an individual hole is the number of strokes it should take a player to get the ball in the hole. A score that matches par for the course is **even par**. If you score even par for eighteen holes you have played every hole in regulation.)

Perspective

The clearest way I can give you this point is to remind you that someone is always having a worse day than you are. This is true in life just as much, if not more so, than on the golf course.

Now, there are going to be some unbelievably bad days in your life. I wish again that I could spare you the pain of them. I also want to tell you that in most cases, things are not as bad as they seem. When adversity occurs we have a tendency to lose perspective of the big picture. Also, in time, an event that seemed terrible at the start can lead to something incredible. Your mom and I had the worst blind date on record—a truly horrible experience for both of us! Were it not for your

Uncle Joe neither one of us would have agreed to a second date. The results fifteen years later are truly spectacular.

There are some exceptions to this attitude, however. The loss of a loved one tops the list of worst times in a person's life that don't offer a silver lining.

Each of us deals with these tragedies differently, some far better than others. It's important to think of other people during this time. A lesson I have learned in my life is that you can heal your wounds faster by immersing yourself in helping someone else. I'm not saying to ignore the raw grief you will feel. Just be aware that sometimes stepping outside of your head can aid the healing process as well.

An excellent illustration of this comes with a story of a time I didn't do so well in this effort. I know this book seems like a top ten list of my worst transgressions, but the point is that I have learned more from my mistakes than my victories.

The time I have in mind was, without a doubt, the worst period of my life. Your mother and I had been married for about four months when we got the news that your Grandpa Jack had suffered a heart attack and was in a coma. The prognosis was not good. He had been without oxygen for too long and the damage to his brain was extensive. Words do not accurately express what he meant to me. I will hope it's enough to say here that he was like a true father to me. When it was time to say our good-byes to him, knowing that he probably didn't even know we were there, I told myself that he was already in a better place.

During this time, your mother and I began to try to make a baby. It was the logical progression for us, since we were so in love. Unfortunately, what should have been quite an easy task proved to be difficult for both of us.

Shortly after that time, we lost your great-grandmother, which was another blow to an already aching heart. Her name was GG, like Gigi, but we used the letters. She was an amazing woman. She and I used to talk politics. We genuinely enjoyed listening to each other's opinions. Before they were a blip on the radar, she told me to get involved with computers (oops, should have listened). She was savvy, especially for someone coming from her generation. She was the last person in the world you wanted to mess with. I have always been surrounded by strong women.

Your mom and I had two miscarriages during this time period as well. After the second one, we traveled that summer to Michigan to visit your great-aunt Patty and great-uncle Rod. Uncle Rod was "the man." The stories you will hear about him will make him sound like a superhero, crime fighter, and Mother Theresa all rolled into one. I will tell you this much: They are not exaggerated. I lived to hear what would come out of his mouth next. He was hilarious. He was wise. If we were allowed to choose whom to be, I would have chosen to be him.

During our visit in early July, we were having a wonderful time. We were relieved to get away from the doctors and the pressure and pain of losing people we loved. We relaxed and had two days with Uncle Rod before *he* died.

I'd like to be clinical about this and classify my feelings about losing someone so full of life so suddenly, but I can't. I *can* describe what it's like to blow air into his lungs, while alternately pumping his chest and willing his heart to beat again. I can say that Uncle Rod went out to ski that day, and that after they brought his body back on the boat, after it became clear that nothing we tried was going to work, and after the doctor told us he was gone, I was never the same.

We came home from one of the many visits to the funeral home on the fourth of July. I drove your great-aunt Patty home that night after another bone-weary day. I remember feeling so torn up inside that it hurt just to breathe. At the same time fireworks were lighting the sky. The one thing I didn't think about was that the woman riding next to me, Uncle Rod's widow, was having a worse day than I was.

Each time I returned to "normal life" after the events of those years, I was bitter. And that, my boy, is an understatement. I felt this way even though I had achieved great success in my job, having been made director of golf at a prestigious private club, and I had the wife of my dreams. We were lucky in that we were both healthy and had our families close by, yet I couldn't focus on the positive, something I normally could do with ease.

Every time I had a normal interaction with a member of the club, whether it was to receive a complaint or compliment, it felt hollow and stupid. One day one of my members came to me to complain that one of the bag room attendants had put his club in the wrong slot of his bag. He was genuinely upset.

Normally, I would have laughed this off after I handled the situation. Some members get a wild hair and even though it seems silly to complain about something so small and inconsequential, I smile, nod, and fix the problem. That is my job.

In this case, I did all that, except I didn't laugh about it afterwards. I became enraged. I fumed about it for weeks. How could someone think for one second that a club in the wrong slot could be worth complaining about, with all the pain in this world? We were at war, for God's sake. People were dying every day. Why didn't people get it?

See, I thought I was the only one who "got it." In actuality, I wasn't keeping my perspective. That may have been one of the stupidest complaints I have ever encountered, but it mattered to that person. If I didn't want to join the living and do my job then someone would do it for me and I would lose even more than I already had.

Around that time, your mother showed me that blue plus sign again. For the first time we made it past some big hurdles in pregnancy terms. Without a doubt, nothing put life in perspective for me like watching you grow inside your mother. As I was thinking of you and her more than myself, I began to heal.

Now I can sum up how to keep perspective on the golf course rather succinctly. Don't be an ass when you're losing; someone has always performed worse than you have. Don't be an ass when you're winning, either. That same person you beat yesterday could kick your ass today.

I want to share a particularly wonderful story about perspective. During my time as director of golf at a private club during the Men's Club Championship, an interesting thing happened. Halfway through the final round, a member collapsed on the ninth green; he was leading the tournament. I happened to be there and called 911. We settled him in my cart and waited for the ambulance. It didn't look good.

The gentleman was rushed to the hospital. The diagnosis was a stroke. It was touch and go, but it looked like he was going to make it. Unfortunately, there was still golf to be played. A winner had to be announced.

Back at the course, I was taught once again that golf is a ladies and gentlemen's game. The three men who were playing with the member who had collapsed all asked what they needed to do to crown the victim as the champion. Thus, they all withdrew from the event.

A few weeks later, we all went to the rehab facility to present him with the trophy of club champion. It was a moving moment. I was taught perspective yet again. There are more lessons to be learned on the golf course than those from winning or losing. These points in life have an underlying message for everyone. One minute you can be the leader in a golf tournament and the next in an ambulance on the way to the hospital with a massive stroke. Another ten minutes later and the man would have been dead. It is so important not to take any moment for granted. In that instant in the rehab facility the trophy meant so little but for the friends that surrounded him and the celebration of his life. With the right teachers on the course, you can learn everything; that includes how to be a good human. Remembering to keep perspective is imperative both on and off the course.

By the way, the member who had the stroke eventually played again with the benefit of a handicapped golf cart. I like to think that he recovered because of the love of his family and friends, along with his passion to get back out on the course.

LESSON 4

*Because your father loves statistics, now would be a good time to tell you that more than two-thirds of all shots take place within one-hundred yards of the green. That being said, I will now cover the next shot as we get farther from the hole: the **pitch shot**.*

There are certainly other shots that are used inside one-hundred yards, but most are specialty shots that *are generally utilized so you can save par or avoid, as your mother says, "the monster numbers," otherwise known as **double bogey** or higher. (A double bogey is a score of two shots over par on any particular hole. For example, on a five-par hole the player shoots a seven. A **bogey** is a score of one shot over par on an individual hole. For example, a player shoots a five for a par-four hole.)*

The pitch shot is where I introduce the second lever. This shot is almost identical to the chip shot, except in the use of the wrists. The wrists are used for this shot and all full swings to help create more clubhead speed which allows us to hit the ball farther and higher, and create more spin.

Although I am talking about using your wrists, keep in mind that too much can be a bad thing. (This is probably true about everything except love and respect—see Chapters 1–9.)

The ball position is in the back of the stance when chipping and pitching but not when putting. A key in pitching is to keep the clubhead low, using the shoulders to start and the wrists near the top of the backswing; the extent, of course, is going to vary depending on how far you hope to hit the ball.

***Always** make sure the grip of the club stays against the palm of your leading hand.*

Don't Be an Asshole

I am sure there is a less crude way of saying this, but nothing rings true for me when I word it differently. It simply sums up how I feel. An appropriate attitude saves you from both being and looking like an idiot during your life.

Think about it. If you keep this phrase in your head as a personal mantra, it could save you hugely in terms of embarrassment, regret and, ultimately, unhappiness.

I first heard this phrase from your Auntie Jess, and while I had told myself variations of it throughout my life, she summed it up perfectly when we approached a rotary in downtown Boston.

Your mother was driving and she was a bit nervous at the prospect of navigating through the aggressive northern drivers (no offense to half of my family). Your aunt very clearly said, "Don't be an asshole Jill, get this right."

Not exactly Shakespeare, but direct enough to have your mother straightening her shoulders and acting accordingly. I have found that no matter the situation, if you tell yourself these four words before you react, most of the time, you'll behave with class, respect, and humility. These are big ones to me as far as important character traits go. I may not always achieve them, but I sure as hell make doing so my goal.

It might seem silly to equate driving around a rotary with a life mantra like this one, but even the little things matter. Had your mother not sucked it up and driven well, we may have ended up in an accident.

The biggest reward reaped from this behavior is genuine friendship. No one worth hanging out with desires the company of an asshole.

That's not to say that people don't associate with them. Sometimes it's inevitable (a certain past manager of mine springs to mind). Usually people won't choose to be with one, unless forced. Sometimes you might not even recognize that you are behaving like one. Don't worry; people have a way of shaking these types loose. You'll know it soon enough and if not, I will have the unfortunate job of pulling you off to the side to let you know. You better hope it's me. I'd hate to see your mother do it. She's a bit more direct than I am.

Some good examples of being an asshole are making a situation all about you; drinking excessively and getting loud (which is very embarrassing to your mother); lying in any form, especially about someone else; acting with cocky arrogance that isn't a joke; being lazy; and not accepting responsibility for your actions.

Of course, these are not the only examples, but they leap out at me immediately. Like I said before, you'll know if you are behaving this way. There is always one in a pack of guys. I absolutely hope it isn't you.

One specific example I can give you of when I was an idiot on the course shines through my past. Yet again, I am faced with the struggle to tell you the truth or to let you think that I am infallible. I will go with the former because it's vital that we are honest with each other. So yes, I was an asshole on the golf course. More than once I am ashamed to admit I was not the ambassador or the gentleman I should have been. In this particular

instance I was playing in a high school tournament against a rival school. A junior on the other
team was nicknamed "Rulebook" for constantly
trying to call individuals on rules violations. (We
weren't that creative with nicknames back then.)
Sure enough, he caught me as I leaned up against
my seven-iron while in a hazard. (Rule: A player
must not touch the ground in the hazard or water
in the water hazard with his hand or a club.) It was
an honest mistake. No, this was not my asshole
moment. That came later. I was embarrassed for
being called out for a mistake I made. Instead of
accepting the penalty gracefully at that point, I
chose to find a way to retaliate. This isn't the usual
way I operate. Not then or now. But that particular
day something came over me and I let my inner
moron loose.

Don't misunderstand me; I believe we have
rules for a reason and I vehemently uphold them
now. But at this time, instead of competing and
concentrating on my own game, I changed my
focus to pay sole attention to someone else in the
hopes that he would fail. I was a real idiot that
day. How stupid is that? I thought I needed that
guy to fail for me to feel good about myself. That
is the epitome of being an asshole on the golf
course. In the end, I caught the kid in his own

rules violation and momentarily felt vindicated. But at what cost? Neither one of us won the tournament. The only thing at stake other than the competition were our reputations as gentlemen on the course which took major hits that day. If you can rise above the pettiness in situations, I highly recommend it. I speak from experience when I say the alternative doesn't allow you to feel that great about yourself.

Now, on to the good stuff: talking about my best friends. While the rest of this chapter may seem like a ringing endorsement of my character, it is more about what not being an ass (most of the time) can get you in return. As I said, I have behaved like one on several occasions. I just have tried not to make it my life's work.

Real friendship is lasting. It's strong and can elevate your life experiences to levels that would not have been achievable were it not for the allies around you. There also will be the middle school "best friends for life" type of relationship. These connections come and go. They are valuable and will always teach you something if you allow yourself to learn.

Best friends, however, are rare. Being one and keeping one takes a lot of work. It means caring about what happens to the other person and being honest with that person. Massive amounts of sympathy and empathy are required, and above all, you have to "get" each other.

Your mother and I count ourselves lucky to call each other best friends and mean it. We are luckier still to have siblings who play this role. Your mother often remarks that having three sisters and a brother growing up meant she was never in need of companionship. Our parents hammered home the point that our brothers and sisters would be the best friends we would ever have in this world and not to forget it; that no matter what kind of fights we got into or disagreements we had, we needed to work things out. As kids we didn't believe it. We wanted to do whatever we could to get away from them. Our siblings kind of had to love us. Your mom and I are blessed that their forced love blossomed into genuine closeness as we became adults.

Taking all the built-in pals away, there are still a very small handful of people I would call my best friends. I like to believe these wonderful people hang out with me because on most days I am not an ass. Whether or not this is true, I am lucky to know them, and the lessons I have learned from each has been invaluable.

These men are so important to me that I made

them all fly to New Hampshire and stand up for me at my wedding to your mother. I have known each of them for at least ten years, most almost twenty. One I have known since I was in elementary school.

These are the people I would call to drive me home if I'd had too much to drink, the ones I would have bail me out of jail (thank God there has been no need for that). They have attended my family funerals. They would drop everything for me at my first request. They are what I define as "best friends."

I would like to think that they think of me the same way. I can't be sure. Some of us are too manly to talk about such things, but I know that no matter what, I am not alone in this world. Knowing this means everything.

I want you to learn to cultivate this kind of ally. You know all of these men because they are important in my life. Some are even family members. I am naming them and the blessings each one brings to my life. For all, I give thanks. I do this here so you will recognize the qualities to look for when you come across your own best friends.

These are mine: Jim Redmile for his kindness and loyalty, Uncle Michael for his understanding and loyalty, Uncle JoJo (your mother's brother Joe) for his sense of family and loyalty, Uncle Ret for his commitment and loyalty, Bob Cheesman for his nonjudgmental nature and loyalty, your cousin Jeffrey for his sense of humor and loyalty, and Kelly Hall for his honesty and loyalty.

Do you see the theme?

These men are true to me and I am to them. Loyalty is a big deal in friendships and in life. Plato thought that only the just could be loyal. The philosopher Josiah Royce believed that loyalty was the supreme moral good and that devotion to an object mattered more than the merits of the object itself. You see, being devoted to a friend is more of a reflection of personal ethics than of the worthiness of the friend in question.

In case you missed it, I am the friend in question in this scenario. So if we use the two philosophers above as a standard (and why wouldn't we?), I have chosen my friends well because not only are they loyal, but they are also ethical. They are devoted to me—even if on occasion I am an asshole (again, I want to shoot for not making *that* a habit).

Let's take it one step further; these men don't cheat, they play fair, they practice the Golden Rule, and they offer perspective. Perhaps you are getting why they are so important in my life, as they live the morals I strive for every day. These are the lessons I hope you learn in your life. These are the kinds of friendships I want you to seek in your life. Surrounding yourself with these kinds of people will only help you on your own journey.

It may be an unfair fact of life that you are judged by the company you keep, but there it is. You are, whether you like it or not. If you look for friends who are loyal, they will always have your back. You can't ask for more than that.

This lesson is such an all-encompassing message that in applying it further to the golf course, I can only point out the obvious: If you have these types of friends, you will never be at a loss for a playing partner. If you are lucky, you'll be able to get a foursome together.

LESSON 5

Practice is quite a big deal to me. I've talked about giving it one-hundred percent. (See Chapter 3.) Here I'll touch on the importance of making sure you are practicing the right things (which is vital in anything that you do). In golf, as I have already discussed, about two-thirds of all shots are within one-hundred yards of the hole. So how much of your time do you think you should spend on these shots, if you are serious and love the game? That's right, two-thirds!

These "right things" can change from session to session. They guide you in both where to spend your time as well as how to spend it. Practice time also provides you with the opportunity to identify a shot or two that you are very confident in so that you can play to these yardages during your rounds. I never took the time to work on these shots because it wasn't "cool" and fun like trying to hit the driver over the fence at the Brooksville Golf & Country Club was. As I wrote before, the short game is what makes champions.

Here is a drill for your practice time. Place trash barrels out fifty, seventy-five, and one-hundred yards away and hit twenty-five balls to each one every session. Don't think that you are only successful if you hit one into the trash can; it is very difficult to hit one into the barrel, and keep in mind that the tour average from seventy-five to one-hundred yards is about sixteen feet. Just like every other shot in golf, keep mental notes of where you are hitting it.

Your One Superpower

Of the nine lessons in this book, you will find this one has a little spot in each. Every person has one superpower. At least, that is how I refer to it. This treasure is the same for everyone. It isn't special, but it is super. It doesn't always get used, but it is always available. You may have guessed that I am referring to the power you possess in your own mind.

While I am a vehement believer in the power of positive thinking, I am not merely referencing that most awesome human ability. I am speaking more to your mind's ability to control your reactions to outside forces. This is the true superpower.

Everyone will be a victim of some wrong in

life. Again, I only wish a father could spare his son this pain. I will pray every day that any misfortune that might befall you be temporary and not life altering. More importantly, I will wish that you use your mind to control and to handle whatever reactions you have when faced with these crises. You have the strength to stop yourself from further becoming a victim. You have the ability to compose your reactions any way you want. You have the power.

Never let me hear you say, "I couldn't help it," because you can. It won't always feel that way, but you absolutely can. I need to repeat it again. You *really can*. Try.

This power can be applied in many ways. No, strike that—in all ways. There isn't a time in your life that you shouldn't use this ability. Use this capacity for good, my son. You will be mocked, you will be bullied, and you will be made to feel small. On the flip side, you will feel exuberant, you will feel free, and you will feel like a big man. In all of these instances, throughout your life, use the gift of your mind to school your reactions appropriately.

We are judged by both our words and actions. Let your mind thoughtfully rule both so that the lessons I have outlined here in this book guide you. Stop before reacting to outside forces and ask yourself some serious questions. Where would I like to be on the other end of this situation? How would I like to be regarded? Am I being an ass? Am I being fair? What if I was in the other person's place? Do I have the proper perspective?

Use your mind, that one superpower, to answer these questions before you react and you should be alright. I can't promise anything, except that by doing so you will retain your self-respect, which should be your long-term goal.

I am not telling you to be bloodless and robotic. I wouldn't want you to be guided in this direction. I like emotions. They are messy, but they are the meat of our existence. I am not saying that I am never overcome with feelings because I am, I have been and I will be again. I just try to respond to situations wisely. That is all I can ask from you.

I give you a two-pronged example. On the one hand, when first faced with the challenge, I reacted poorly and my actions reflect that. As time went on, I learned how to harness this power and used it well. I am now proud of how it all turned out.

One of my first jobs outside of Brooksville was as a "cart guy" at a nice public club. The place was busy. Crazy busy. I was enjoying the tip money a lot, and I was working my way up to outside manager. Being in my early twenties, I thought I was well on the right career path. Two things happened that made me reevaluate. Strike that; two *people* happened.

I was the best worker in the cart barn at the time. Then we got a new director of golf (DOG). This dude was for real, or so we thought. He was supposed to be incredible. He was to certain people, depending on his mood or how important the other person could be to his advancement. He could be outrageously funny, but his humor could turn into biting sarcastic comments so quickly it would make my twenty-something head spin. I lost sleep over this man. My relationships suffered. I am not proud.

This fellow also liked to party. A lot. There is nothing wrong with that exactly, it just pertains to the end of the story. Stay tuned. I thought for a while that I should emulate him. You can probably guess this person didn't have the time of day for me. He spent more time making jokes at the expense of others (me included) than actually managing. "Ineffective" would be an excellent word to describe him. It soon came out that he had been fired from his other job. Some of the other workers and I started to realize that he wasn't all he was cracked up to be.

But boy, did he have an effect on some of us for a while, as being in our twenties we were hungry for some approval. Maybe even some mentoring would have been nice from a boss of his supposed caliber. We didn't get it from this guy. If he ever got it into his head to be a guide to someone, I pity the resulting golf professional. Eventually he belittled everyone below him at the course. Morale was low.

After a while, that sandpaper personality began to grate on me. As soon as the DOG realized that there was less hero worship and more questioning, he became more of an invisible boss than he had been before. These elusive leaders are never there when an employee needs them. They offer no mentoring. They are always around when prominent members are around, but do not consider employee issues important at all. They are hard to pin down, won't commit to returning correspondence in writing and never return phone calls to employees. They can easily blame their employees for screw-ups and happily take the credit for victories and for work done while they weren't around.

This guy was the perfect example of every

bad stereotype you hear about golf pros. He was lazy and only wanted to play golf for a living. He wasn't a good manager. He couldn't make it on tour so he tried to stay in the golf world by working in country clubs even though he didn't love the work. He was more interested in partying than anything else. He had a personality like a car salesman when he was hustling lessons. It is a shame that there are pros like this out there.

Further, it is a shame that I allowed myself to care so much about what this man thought. I never used my superpower once. I lost who I was and bought into his terrible self-serving antics for a while. I wouldn't put myself out for anyone unless something was in it for me. I was only interested in what I wanted to do when I wanted to do it. I only cared about people who could do something for me or advance my career.

It was not good. I didn't see at the time that this boss of mine had no superpower at all. He was insecure, overly competitive, and looked at every man he met as a potential threat, even a lowly (in his estimation) cart guy such as me. It took me a while to shake loose the bad feelings he evoked in me. I am not proud that I didn't use the strength of my mind to put him in the category to which he belonged. That category is DOES NOT

MATTER WHAT THEY THINK. Remember it well, my son. More than a lot of people will fall into this group.

During this time, the second person to make me reevaluate my career path came into my life in the form of a new cart guy. Since I was the best (or so I was told) it was my job to train him on how to clean carts. Cart cleaning is not exactly saving the world, but it's a job, so it is important to do it well, as you would everything else in life.

I was quite curious about this guy's story. He was a few years older than I was and he was good. Too good. If I showed up at four a.m., he was there fifteen minutes earlier. If I cleaned forty carts in a day, he cleaned five more. I was really annoyed. The trouble with his behavior was that he wasn't doing it *to* me. He was doing it for the same reason I was—because he believed in doing the job right. The real irritation was that he was better than I was.

I became competitive. I might have even become a bit insufferable for a while. But the greatest part of the story is that because of that man, I tried, even harder than I had before. We ran neck and neck almost every day and because of him that was one of the best times of my life. The reason? This person was not an asshole. (See

Chapter 5.) He was the antithesis. At that point, I didn't realize his charisma was on a level I had never encountered and that he used his powers for good, unlike the boss we had at the time. Seriously, this fellow could run for office against Bill Clinton and most likely win. He just sucked me into his world and made every effort to befriend me. It worked.

I discovered that while he was at an age when most people are finding success in their chosen careers, he had decided to chuck it all and have a go at golf, as it had always been his passion. This gamble was such a strange concept to me. I didn't come from a place that would encourage such a risk, but as I explain in another chapter, there is nothing wrong with pursuing a dream; I just didn't realize it at the time.

Anyway, this person had quit a very lucrative job where he was making more money than most head golf pros to be a cart guy. This wasn't just a simple pay cut. He left a safe world that he was comfortable in for a foreign career path with little-to-no guarantees for success. This was a huge deal. He used his superpower to change his life path and he didn't let anyone sway him on his way.

He spent *years* practicing for the P.A.T. (the Player Ability Test), the aptitude requirement for entry to the Professional Golf Management program administered by the PGA. The requirement is to play thirty-six holes in the same day. You must shoot within fifteen shots of the course rating (e.g., for a course with a rating of 70.0 per round - so 140 - plus the fifteen shots, you must shoot at least 155). This evaluation has a similar pass rating as that of the Bar and CPA exams.

A few times, this individual didn't pass the P.A.T. but he didn't give up until finally he did. He became a general manager. As I said before, he was just that good. He was a mentor. In many ways, he was a hero to me. He *kept* trying. He taught me to use my power for good.

By the way, that guy? He's your Uncle JoJo. I believe he came into my life for two reasons. One was so I could learn the superpower lesson from him, and the other was so I could meet your mother and have you. This is absolutely a true story. Uncle Joe is the real thing. The other character I described was just an insecure wannabe dressed in a confident wolf's clothing.

Now let's skip ahead almost twenty years. I saw that old boss of mine for the first time in years and wouldn't it have to be on one of the biggest nights of my life? I was being honored with an award at the PGA annual meeting. More importantly, I was going to meet Arnold Palmer, my first golf hero. You might have guessed that your middle name has something to do with him.

Both your mother and I have strong feelings about naming children after celebrities. We are against it. It sets the kid up for all kinds of comparisons and could lead to delusions of grandeur. However, Arnold Palmer is not only a celebrity but also a true gentleman. He was the first ambassador for the game I love. He is a good sport. He has integrity. He didn't throw his clubs and he doesn't disrespect anyone. He always uses the superpower for good. All in all, your mother and I thought that if we were going to name you after anyone, he would be our first choice, after your Grandpa Jack (another hero of mine).

Anyway, back to the night in question. Arnold Palmer was amazing. The meeting was everything I had hoped for. The king schooled me yet again. His speech was moving. He spoke of what I consider most important in golf: no matter who you are, as he put it, "don't be an ass." He was witty and direct. Above all, when I met with him he was gracious. He does not have to be any of those things. Some might say he has earned the right to sit in his house and relax, that he owes no one anything. Yet, he makes these appearances, mingles with the pros and makes the speeches because even at eighty-one years old, he knows that what essentially matters is being an ambassador for the game and a gentleman.

Afterwards, while I was still riding the high of the day, I was speaking to a rather important man in the PGA ranks when my ex-boss joined the conversation. At this time in his life, he was considered quite powerful. He was a big deal. In no time at all, he belittled me in front of the other PGA member by describing me as a twenty-something party animal with no direction or drive, ironic given his proclivities for partying. Again, I don't have a problem with people having a good time, I just don't like it when they throw stones. At that moment, I was back there in that little cart barn, feeling those horrible feelings of inadequacy. I was mad enough that my jaw cracked and my fists clenched. But I stopped. I was forty years old. I had worked my butt off to earn the award I had been presented. I was just as important as this fellow, and moreover, I was a nice human. I used my one superpower and said only this, "Obviously, you have the wrong guy."

I walked away and never heard from him again. More importantly, I didn't think about him again. He did not ruin my night. Having control of your reactions means just that. It doesn't mean standing there and taking it. To react effectively, you must know that this type of person isn't worth losing control over. Ever.

Try to remember the above lesson, and that if you lose your superpower, then you have given that power to someone else. You have lost the only control you have and given it away to an outside force. Strive never to let this happen. Nothing is worth losing this most important strength. No person is either. Use your mind to be positive and effective.

When applying your one superpower to the golf course, it is paramount that you think before you react. Nothing ruins a round of golf more than having a hothead throw his clubs and scream at himself after every bad shot. (I will expound on this reaction in the next chapter.) You may lose. You may stink that day or you may shoot the course record, but no matter what, you can be powerful and positive in your mind.

Stroke play, or *medal play,* is when players add up all of the strokes taken during the course of the round. Whoever has the lowest number wins. In *match play,* the player that bests his opponent on a hole earns a point for the hole no matter how many strokes it takes to win the hole. You will need to use your superpower to guide you, especially in match play. You cannot allow other influences such as your competitor's attitude or game to affect yours. Distractions such as heckling, a bird singing, or the fact that your mother is watching can get into your head only if you allow them. Use your mind to block it all out. Only focus on playing your game. Needless to say, real power and control in life and on the course are fleeting and are often myths. The only place you have these capacities is in your mind.

LESSON 6

*Your posture and set up on the full swing are perhaps the most important factors in the golf swing. There is an old acronym in golf called **GAP: grip, address, and posture**. These three items together make it simpler to play consistent golf at any level.*

*The easiest way to take the **grip**, I find, is to take the forward hand, go to shake hands with it and place it on the club so the back of that hand is facing the target and slightly up from that line. There are two other keys to having this hand in the correct position. They are first to make sure the grip goes under the "fat" of the hand, which is more across than up and down the palm, and then to ensure the line between the index finger and thumb are pointing toward the back shoulder.*

Now take the back hand (the hand farther from the target) and do the same thing. This hand should go on with the palm facing the target and the line between the index and thumb pointing to the same shoulder.

The **address** is the way you set up to the golf ball. The key is to have your feet, knees, hips, and shoulders all parallel to the target line. Being the correct distance from the ball, where your arms will hang straight down from your shoulders, is also essential, allowing you to keep your arms relaxed.

The **position** of the ball between the feet is also fairly important. Have the ball in the middle of the stance when the ball is on the ground, and near the forward heel when the ball is teed up. The club will reach its lowest point in the middle of the swing, allowing you to take a divot with your irons. When the ball is on a tee, you'll be able to catch it on the way up. You see, the club travels on an arc. Irons are played in the middle of the stance to hit the ball at the bottom of the arc. The ball is past the bottom of the arc when it is on a tee so, in this case, you can hit it on the way up (the upswing).

Finally, focus on your **posture**. Be sure that your spine is nice and straight. It may feel like you are sticking your butt out, but that is correct. Now, even though your spine is straight from top to bottom, it is also tilted toward the ball and slightly away from the target. The posture is very important, since now all you have to do is rotate around the spine without any lateral movement.

Temper, Temper

Unfortunately, this is one lesson with which I am all too familiar. There are just too many times in a person's life that brainless behavior can accompany anger. Whether or not the feeling is justified is beside the point. Violent, irrational behavior is never justifiable.

I'm not saying you should never get mad, because you will. What I am suggesting is that, just as I advised in the last lesson, you can do your best to react in a dignified manner. If that fails and it probably will at some point, please apologize profusely, genuinely, and without equivocation. And again, try.

The first question anyone should ask himself

when he becomes angry with a person or situation is this: Is my emotion worth it? What is "it," you say? You have to ask if the anger you feel is worth huge embarrassment, irrevocable relationship changes, or even potential incarceration, as well as regret, low self-esteem or stress-related issues. Then, as I have learned from your grandfather, invoke the *twenty-four-hour rule*—wait that long before confronting or reacting to the person who made you so angry. If doing this doesn't work, then go forty-eight hours. Then, if you are still upset, be direct, be calm, and try to see it from the other side. Approach the situation or person calmly and with control.

I'd like to tell you that this method will resolve all your conflicts and every person you meet will be impressed with your inner strength. That just isn't the case and I surely don't want to mislead you. I'd also like to tell you that you won't be so mad in your life that tears spring to your eyes and it feels as if your blood is boiling. But I can't. You will be this mad, I am sure, plenty of times. You will want to punch something. Please try very hard not to.

I can speak so well to this lesson because I have been there. The results were less than desirable, to say the least. Admitting this weakness for such a stupid reason as I am about to reveal is hard, especially to my son. But it happened, so there it is. I promised I wouldn't lie plus I'd actually like you to get something from this book, so here goes.

When I was a young man in my teens and early twenties, I was a hothead. I don't know where this temper came from exactly, but it seems that ultimately the explanation for outrageous conduct for this demographic is that "boys will be boys." I hate this excuse for several reasons. Stereotypical behavior is not generally acceptable. I have had twenty years to think about this and I now know that we should strive for an existence above the fray of average expectations. In addition, this mentality usually gives young men an excuse to behave badly, especially in sports.

As an aside, I want to get across to you that talent of any kind is a gift. Brains, coordination, the ability to swing a bat or club, and a mind that could earn a Nobel Prize are all blessings. They are also a huge responsibility, not excuses to behave badly. Tantrums, snobbery, arrogance, and generally acting intolerably are not justifiable in any case, even if you are Tiger Woods. When you are exceptionally talented at something, your life takes on a dimension most people can't wrap their minds around. Yes, it's hard, but you are also unbelievably fortunate. Whether you like it or not, you are an example to everyone around you. If you are gifted in some way try to remember how lucky you are and, most importantly, that you are a role model. Conduct yourself like a gentleman. When people with outstanding ability act poorly, the excuse most often cited is that these wunderkinds need to blow off steam because of the incredible strain they are feeling. I don't buy it. You are not entitled to special treatment. If you can't handle the pressure, don't do it. I realize this is a harsh approach, but I feel strongly about this. So there it is. If you need to rant, take a vacation. Don't vent at people who didn't ask for it and definitely don't deserve it.

Now, I'll turn back to my own hotheadedness and some of the times it led to embarrassment and an overwhelming feeling of stupidity (even as I remember them now). In these instances, I was lucky it didn't flare up more than it did. Anger can easily escalate, inevitably leading to regret. Avoiding grief over past choices in life is a struggle. You won't accomplish this feat, but you can try to control the occasions when your temper leads you to it.

When I was around twenty, I was playing

darts with a group of guys in a bar. It should come as no surprise that alcohol played a major role in the events of the evening. Now, my son, I will not be hypocritical, and tell you to be a teetotaler. I believe booze can and should be enjoyed responsibly. Part of adult responsibility is knowing your limits. Too much drink has a tendency to erase the limits *in your mind only.* They still exist in reality; you just lose the ability to *recognize* when to stop behaving badly. That is not to say I condone the catchall excuse "but I was drunk" which is never an acceptable reason for poor behavior.

Another thing too much alcohol can do to a body is enhance feelings such as anger, fear, and happiness—this can be very dangerous. The night in question is a perfect example of this. The dart game we were playing intensified as the evening went on and we began betting on the results. The beer was flowing, and the machismo even more so. One thing led to another and I lost my temper. Unfortunately, I was the ass on this night. Can you guess the results of my temper over a *dart game?* A broken hand. Yup, I punched a dartboard because I didn't like a shot I made or the subsequent comments by my buddies.

Beyond stupidity, this act is at the very least grounds for a drunken and disorderly charge, possibly even an intentional destruction of property arrest. I was lucky. I only damaged my hand and pride. Keeping a cool head is a much higher ideal. Again, I am not condoning passionless living. But when you find yourself in this kind of situation, please attempt to "skip ahead," as they say, and see where you'll come out on the other side if you let hotheadedness rule. Odds are you'll be pleased with the results if you let the anger go and logic prevail. No rational reason exists as to why I should have had a broken hand at the end of a night of "fun with friends." Bad tempers and stupidity walk hand in hand. Try to remember that.

The next couple of examples carry the lesson to the links. I'll start with telling you about the one and only time I threw a club on the course. I was in a tri-county junior event when I was about sixteen. I had just bought the first clubs I had ever paid for myself. My mother was watching me play. I hit a terrible shot on a par five. I threw my seven-iron after hooking one into the woods. The club landed *high* in a huge oak tree, at least fifty feet up. My mother said nothing. I was unable to get to the club so I was without it the rest of the tournament. After I lost the event, my mom sent me back to get the iron. My buddies and I got it out with sheer luck by throwing other clubs at it, finally knocking it loose. When I got home, my mother asked me to bring her my golf bag. She took my clubs and put them in her closet. She told me that I needed to decide if I indeed wanted to be a professional golfer and respect the game or behave like a juvenile idiot. She gave me a month without my clubs to make the decision. Needless to say, it was a long and painful punishment for someone who practiced every day. More importantly, it was a much-needed lesson in self-control which I continued to learn as I grew up.

Another time I lost out due to my temper on the golf course was when I was nineteen. I was working at a nice club managing the cart barn. Each Wednesday, its president would ask me to play with him and two members. This was a nice thing to be asked to do, and I was genuinely pleased. I found out later that one of the major reasons he asked me to play was because of my ability. The pressure was on me each week, as I obviously wanted to be great. However, after a few times of playing with me, the club president stopped issuing the invitation.

My head pro brought me into his office and explained that the president loved my swing. He also thought I had great potential and a terrific sense of humor. However, after playing with me for a few weeks he couldn't put up with my "temper tantrums" anymore because it made playing eighteen holes uncomfortable. Yikes.

Not only was this extremely humiliating news, but my head pro also told me that he had been considering bringing me in the shop a couple days a week to start learning the ropes of the inside operation. Instead, because of the information the club president had relayed to him, he realized I needed more time outside to "grow up." Yikes again.

So, because I couldn't control my outrage after making some bad shots on the course, I lost a weekly game with a nice man and a potential promotion—an excellent but very painful lesson. I can't say I began to mellow immediately but I did put a lid on my temper and try to control myself. I started to realize (as I outlined in Chapter 6) that I have the power to control my reactions. I wasn't going to let my temper cost me anything else in the future.

Other illustrations of my message here are the disgusting displays of temper from touring professionals like Tiger Woods and Sergio Garcia when they spit on the fairway or in the cup after a bad shot. Indeed, there are plenty of stories of pros throwing clubs or swearing. Such outbursts can lead to heavy fines for the player and an even heavier hit to their reputations as both ambassadors to the game and as gentlemen.

LESSON 7

Jax, your greatest strength in the game is yet to be determined, but as your father, a PGA member, and bit of a gambler, I'm going to guess that it is going to be the length of your shot. Although there are no guarantees, length is probably the most difficult to teach. However, efficiency is very teachable and has a lot to do with **tempo**. *(An individual's tempo is like a fingerprint. Some people do things at a very fast pace while others are simply slower.)*

Efficiency is the ability to get the most power with the highest amount of control. How do you do it? The biggest factor is making sure all of your angles stay intact. "What angles?" you ask. The forward arm (the one closer to the target) stays fully extended and creates a ninety-degree angle with the shaft of the club. Too much momentum causes a breakdown in these angles (your forward arm bending at the elbow or going too far beyond the ninety-degree angle I just talked about) during the backswing.

You will hear golf instructors and amateurs often say "slow down" or "swing easy." These generic statements fail to convey the reason. If you go too fast on the way back, you create such momentum that you cannot stop the clubhead at the top of the swing and it continues to go back as you go to start the forward swing. When you do this, you will without a doubt create a breakdown in one of those angles. Whatever you do, **do not think about going slower!** If you simply slow down, you are losing your tempo and it may not remain coordinated with your personality.

A better way to maintain your angles is physically to feel something, anything! Yeah, it sounds a little silly, but if you focus on your body doing something, then you can get your mind off all the negative issues, such as where **not** to hit the ball, as your mind is taken to a positive place. The one thing that I have found to be very effective is the same aspect I discussed while pitching; feel the palm of the forward hand stay against the grip of the club. If this doesn't happen, the club will be allowed to go beyond the ninety-degree mark in relation to the forward arm. When the club comes off that palm, you lose control. The only way to regain that control is to re-grip the club, which will cause us to lose that ninety-degree angle, and thus your angle to the ball and a great portion of your clubhead speed. Too much work and speed causes a loss of power and a lack of efficiency. This is what often happens when players hit the ball too hard.

Opinions

Opinions are funny things, my son. To illustrate this idea, let's use this book as an example. Everything in here is my viewpoint, even my versions of the events that I have outlined. Memories are strange, and so when I relay an occurrence that happened in the past, it is clouded by my perspective of the outcome, of who I was when it took place and the people who were involved in it. I have tried to be as factual as possible because I promised I wouldn't lie, but you sometimes can't help those pesky judgments from sneaking in.

Opinions are everywhere. Just please don't buy the line from anyone that they have no viewpoint on any particular matter. Because they do, and while they may not express them all the time (which is often fortunate), they will have them nonetheless. Oftentimes, people will express their perspective to you after you have made a decision and the outcome is unfavorable. I like to call these the "I told you so" ones. Of course they knew that your decision would lead to this misfortune, but they didn't want to butt in. Right. Sure. Uh-huh.

Some express their opinions as suggestions on how to run your life, usually stating their view with the caveat of, "If it were me, I'd do it this way," or some variation to that effect. These perspectives are especially convincing because you have to assume that if someone would do something for themselves a certain way, then they wouldn't be steering you wrong. Sure, I can buy that. Sort of.

Another way people express their opinions, a personal favorite of mine, is by saying nothing at all. But you know...you always know. Your mother is particularly good at this. Knowing her as long as I have, I usually have an excellent idea of what she's thinking anyway. You'll be able to tell as well.

Opinions are appraisals people make in regards to every aspect of their lives. Whom you vote for, whom you marry, which doctor you choose, how you discipline, and how you love are all examples of decisions that require you to make a judgment call, form a viewpoint, and apply it to your life. Even if you're smart and do the proper research, these choices will be difficult to make. You must make them though, as you can't avoid doing so and still have a full life.

You must sense another "but" coming. There is a big one. Research and your own intelligence, and even the views of others, can be excellent tools in forming opinions of your own, but there is one aspect of decision making that many people leave out or ignore completely. That one aspect is your gut. I'm not talking about prime-time detective shows and the rogue cop who operates solely on his "gut feeling." That's silly and fictional. While it might entertain, it seems like a stupid way to live your life.

The gut instinct I am speaking about *is* a feeling deep inside you but one that is based on your ability to read people and situations and pull a message from them. There is always a lesson, Jax. It's your job to figure it out and apply it to your life. As a quick aside, I will tell you that the ability to read people well is a true gift and one at which I wish I excelled. I keep learning and trying, and hope you will, too. Your grandmother Beami is excellent at this, and every day I work to emulate her ability to read below the surface of what people are saying to what people *actually* mean. (More on this in Chapter 9.)

What I am talking about are your instincts. In my opinion (ha ha), too often we teach our children to ignore their gut and instinctive feelings. We tell them not to talk to strangers, but make them say hello to the cashier at the grocery store when she says hello. If our child doesn't perform we get embarrassed or scold him or her. This seems contradictory to me, as a cashier is a stranger to our child in the truest sense of the word. Instincts are important, and more times than I am comfortable with they are ignored. We are animals, after all.

Forming an opinion should be a three-way decision-making process that utilizes all forces available to us: your brain and research, the views of others, and your gut instincts. If you use these three elements, you should win the battle every time. I have struggled with indecisiveness my entire life not wanting to make a misstep. Until meeting your mom I had few opinions and made almost no decisions for fear of making the wrong ones. I am working on it, but that is why I refer to it as a battle.

If you make the wrong choice even after using

all three elements, you misjudged the situation. Big deal. Move on. But not before you learn from the error. The only real mistakes are the ones you don't learn from.

As one giant caveat to the above formula, I will say that the opinions of others should not weigh significantly when forming your own judgments. Try to see the views of others as the whipped cream of life. It's nice, but a little goes a long way and most times you don't need it and won't miss it if it isn't there in the first place.

The whole point of this chapter is that the opinions of others are most important to the people who hold them. They should not become *your* bible. They should always be taken with a grain of salt, as you can't know for sure what the other people's motivations are in sharing them. This may seem cynical, but in reality it doesn't have to be. For example, a mother's thought that her child should not go to college in another state may have more to do with her missing her baby then wanting to control his fate. The decision should be made by the child. His call matters most here. While this is hardly a negative inter-pretation of another person's perspective, that mother's point of view could hold back her son and be damaging to him nonetheless.

Life decisions like these should always be made with your head, your heart, your gut, and lots of research. This study should include querying those whose ideas you respect. It is helpful to gather intelligence from those around you, but again, ultimately, only you will know what is right for you.

I can sum this all up with something I learned from Grampie. The opinions of others matter little. The only views that count are those of the people who will be sitting in the first few rows at your funeral. Of course, your Grampie says it like this, "What do you care? They ain't going to your funeral, are they?" This may seem simplistic, but in actuality, it's genius.

Think about it. This idea frees you from having to worry about what others think. In a perfect world, you will only take into consideration the opinions of those who care about you the most, people who should have your best interests at heart. This lesson should also spill over into that sneaky world of peer pressure. Now, I am not stupid enough to think that you will not fall victim to this overwhelming force. People of all ages want approval. It is human nature. Just try to remember that true happiness comes from being free of the need for anyone's consent and living your life on your own terms. Is this utopian? Yes. I just think it's a nice thing to shoot for.

Before we step into my past again, I want to get one thing across to you. You aren't living on the planet alone. I don't condone ignoring laws and mores, the generally accepted opinions of our current society which change generationally. While I am not a conformist, neither am I a fan of nonconformity. My belief is that if you don't like the way the world works or its viewpoints, you should work within it to make positive changes. That is spoken like a true parent, I know. But I like to think that this idea worked for Gandhi and Martin Luther King, Jr., so it's more than good enough for us. I realize that they broke laws, but they were stupid laws (society eventually agreed), so peaceful civil disobedience was a good, positive way to bring about change.

That is enough on that subject, as I don't consider myself an expert on political thinking and I pray that you avoid the dangers associated with standing up for a cause. I would be proud of you if you did so, but I would be scared for your safety and hope you will avoid danger at all costs. See, this is one of those selfish opinions parents can't help but have. I know without a shadow of a doubt that the loved ones of the gentlemen referenced in the above paragraph would have preferred that these men remained free from harm.

I only know what works for me, and that is the whole point. Find out what works for you and stick to it. You won't always succeed, but I need you to try.

The next story I want to relate to you is entirely true and speaks to one of the single biggest regrets I have, at least in regards to letting another person's opinion shape my decisions and ultimately my life.

As I have related to you in previous chapters, when I was nineteen I was commuting to college. During that time, my attention was focused on golf, but a lot of it was being diverted to other pastimes. Now may be the time for me to confess (although by the time you read this, you will already know) that I love sports. Your mother will contend that I will watch *anything* ESPN broadcasts (and then some). It is likely true. I love the spirit of competition. I love that the games are a metaphor for life. Nothing is more beautiful to me than the journey the players take to the final score. While it isn't politically correct to admit this, I love that there is always a winner and always a loser. Nothing is ever simple, but the outcome of a game is as close to it as you can get. A person can argue bad calls or errors. The bottom line as to why I love athletic competition is this: If you are good enough and if you work hard enough, most times you will end up being victorious. I have not found any other life activity as simply satisfying. It isn't just about winning or losing to me. It isn't about one-hundred million dollar contracts or stacking the deck in your favor (hello, Yankees). It is the fact that anyone, from any walk of life and any demographic, can usually get a fair shake on the field (if they are blessed with the talent). Call me naïve, but I find that dirty refs, juiced athletes, and corporate sponsorships can't mar the inherent beauty of sports.

I can talk about sports forever. One of your mother's biggest pet peeves about me is that while I can recite the starting lineup for the 1984 Detroit Tigers, as well as each player's stats for the year, I oftentimes forget to pick up diapers on my way home from work. She has every right to be annoyed. I have no idea why my mind works like this. It just does. I try to remember the diapers though, and I am much better than I used to be.

With that explanation, you should be able to get a handle on why, to this day, I am so disappointed that I let another person's opinion rule over my dreams and my confidence in myself.

As I was telling you before I was sidetracked, I was going to college and my mind was wrapped up completely in the world of sports. This had been the case since I was roughly six years old. (Remember, I was a late bloomer and hadn't met a girl I wasn't afraid of yet.) When it came time for me to visit the guidance counselor to discuss my career plans and "the future," I shared my deepest hope and biggest dream. First, I wanted to try my hand at being a professional golfer. Then I wanted more than anything to become a sportscaster. I wanted to talk about sports for a living. This was one aspect of my life in which I had complete confidence. Willing to go head to head with any sports expert, I was ready for the advisor to tell me what had to be done to achieve this goal. After all, that was her job.

You can probably guess she didn't jump up and down and shout that I was the next Stuart Scott. (Stuart is a sportscaster and anchor on ESPN SportsCenter. I admire his knowledge and humor. He would have been someone that I would have emulated had I pursued a broadcasting path.) She wasn't even particularly gentle in informing me that my dreams were unrealistic. "Mr. Beckwith," she began. "I can't agree that your aptitudes are well matched for a career in communications, and besides, you don't really have the voice for broad-casting." Ouch. That hurt. She continued, "From your test scores I would point you toward a career utilizing your excellent ability in mathematics. Maybe accounting?"

This brutal response was quite the dream crusher, but only because I allowed her to have merit that she didn't deserve. I rehashed the conversation in my mind for weeks. One of my new favorite pastimes became attempting to deepen my voice, which only resulted in making me sound stupid and giving me a sore throat. I studied every sports anchor I could and finally came up with the idea that she had been right. She must have known what she was talking about. She did this for a living. You see, I came from a small town and believed more or less everything anybody said to me.

After a few weeks of hearing that counselor's voice in my head repeatedly, I put away my wild-est dream to instead pursue something practical. Can you believe it? After *one* lousy opinion, I was finished dreaming. How stupid could I get? But there it is. I can't say I am not disappointed in myself, because I am. Bitterly so. I gave up quickly on something I supposedly wanted more than anything, on the advice of one person who wasn't even an expert in the field I had chosen. This was just stupid.

It's not as though I don't understand why the counselor said what she did. I come from a very practical-minded family. We don't believe in long shots or the lottery. We believe in pensions, benefits and sticking with one company for forty years. This is not a bad way to live. It just doesn't leave a lot of room for dreams. Even after meeting your mother and having her show me that working toward one is worthwhile and not crazy, I have moments of doubt. I have to push myself to remember that Dr. Seuss was rejected twenty-six times before he was published. Had he listened to those first twenty-six opinions and quit working toward his aspiration, the world would be without *Oh, the Places You'll Go!* and *Green Eggs and Ham*.

As with all of these lessons, I can easily apply this one to the golf course. Golf is quite simple, my son, and I love it even for that reason alone. But just as in life, opinions and judgment calls rule on the golf course. Numerous accounts exist of players listening to their partners or caddies on an extremely tough shot and missing. Usually, the reports are followed up with the players saying that they knew they should have done it differently, but they didn't trust their instincts.

These are painful lessons when these decisions cost you a tournament. I am not advocating that you ignore expert opinions, such as those of a caddy, who knows the course backwards. But let me pose this to you: That expert, caddy, or playing partner of yours is not accountable for your score at the end of the round. They aren't signing your scorecard or swinging the club. If your gut instinct tells you something different, don't necessarily ignore it. It probably is the best way for you. Besides, if you miss, you'll have no one to blame but yourself and there is some comfort in that as well.

So I am saying "Go for it, Jax." Who cares what anybody else thinks, anyway? They aren't going to your funeral.

LESSON 8

You're going to have a lot of people give you a lot of advice in golf and in life; be very aware of who you are getting that advice from. One important piece of guidance that I am going to give you will only help you in your game, which is "avoid the big number." The best way to do this is with a good, smart short game. Earlier I mentioned some additional short game specialty shots that can help you score. Here are two big *ones: the **bunker shot** and the **flop shot**.*

These two shots are very similar in a number of ways. Both have you set up open to the target with the club face open then take an outside swing with a wide arc. Both require great stability (meaning no weight shift at all) and a great amount of confidence, as they are shots with big swings to hit the ball a short distance. The mind has trouble grasping this last concept. Always accelerate in these shots; those who lack confidence will decelerate, which will cause a variety of mishits. The one difference in these shots is that with the bunker shot, you do not touch the ball, whereas with the flop, you do (barely). With the bunker shot you are hitting the sand which then hits the ball and propels it out of the sand. When hitting the flop shot, the club is sliding right underneath the ball and barely making contact with the bottom of the ball making it go straight up, high in the air.

Again, let me stress the confidence it takes to pull off either of these shots. To better explain, you have been taking full swings to hit the ball a long distance, and your mind understands this relationship. When you take that big swing and the flag is only a short distance away, your mind can shut down because it doesn't make sense. This is why you need to spend a lot of time practicing both of these shots, so you can get your mind to realize these possibilities.

You Have Nothing to Fear

Your grandmother Beami is an extremely wise woman. By the time you read this, you will be well aware of that fact. I defer to her on several things because she's smart, her life experience is unparalleled, and she has a gift in regards to being able to read people.

Reading people well doesn't just help out the average car salesman. When you can gauge undercurrents to the conversation going on around you or you can tell what a person means rather than what they say, you, my friend, hold the keys to the kingdom. You would be a wise, sensitive person who (if you paid attention to these undercurrents) would be very successful as a friend, employee, boss, person, and so on. However, according to Beami, this is something that can't be taught. You can help someone be more intuitive but only up to a certain point. This is why I am not writing this section on how to read people.

Instead, I will hope against hope that you inherit this gift from your grandmother and use it wisely. I only bring it up because Beami has taught me so much over the years that I use her as an excellent tool to help me when dealing with everyone I meet, but mostly I use her as a mentor for parenting.

You see, Jax, Beami is a goddess of parenting. She will be the first to tell you she has made some off-the-chart blunders as a mother, and her kids will agree. The reason she is so amazing is that she learns from these mistakes and does better the next time. Every single one of her kids will agree she is an outstanding grandmother, and that is all that matters to them now. Beami looks at kids as real people and reads them just as well as she does adults. That, in addition to her experience of helping to raise her younger five siblings, then the five children of her own, and ultimately her five grandkids, makes me defer to her judgment a lot in regards to raising you. When I set about writing this last chapter, I got some perspective from other parents but your grandmother is my guru.

I will begin to talk to you about fear and then, more importantly, regret. I believe fear is natural and instinctive. Beami disagrees. She will grant me fear of the usual suspects, such as snakes and bugs. The rest, she says is taught.

This is a big declaration. A lot of people disagree with her. You are free to do so. It won't change her mind either way. Beami believes that parents are responsible for their children's reactions to the world around them.

Yes, we have the nature-versus-nurture argument. One side says a child's personality is hard-wired from birth, so that sometimes serial killers are just born, not made. The other side of the debate is that a child's personality is shaped by his experiences with those around them. The determining factors come down to genetics or environment. I myself believe that both play a role in the final product, but I'm no expert.

For the most part Beami believes that children *can* blame their parents for how they view the world. She also maintains that after the age of thirty you should have seen enough of the world to stop whining that someone else is responsible for your actions. (Beami can't abide excuses.)

This may seem contradictory, but it's not. Her

theory is that some parents, just by being themselves, can easily screw up their kid's perspectives. But after the kid has been out in the "real world" long enough, he or she should be able to ascertain that there are other ways of viewing the world and mistakes do not have to be repeated.

I can break this theory down to its bare bones by giving an example: Racists are made, not born. Beami's perspective holds true in so many instances. If a person's father is a diehard Yankees fan (God forbid), then even if that person doesn't care very much about baseball, they will probably have warm feelings toward that team because of their dad. Or, let's take the case of an exceedingly nervous kid who worries about everything from the time he is four years old. Five will get you ten that there is a neurotic parent waiting for him at home whose reactions to every germ, meal choice, or potential bedtime ritual are fraught with fear. Of course, exceptions to this rule exist, but for my purposes here I'll let anecdotal evidence reign supreme.

Now I will extrapolate on this theory further into the world of fear and regret. Beami's firm belief after her many years of child-rearing is that children are born fearless. Parents add caution and fear to the child's vocabulary. Caution is necessary at times, but fear is generally unnecessary. Caution is what stops us from walking against the light at an intersection. Fear *stops* us from learning to swim. Fear holds a person back from realizing his dreams. Fear is a four-letter word to your grandmother. Beami knows fear leads to regrets. She does not know how to swim. She waited until she was in her sixties to travel to Europe, due to her fear of flying, and avoids parties because she has a fear of being the center of attention.

The beauty of Beami is that she tried extraordinarily hard not to pass these phobias on to her children. I say that she tried, because you can only do so much when you yourself are so afraid that you avoid situations where you may encounter your fear. According to Beami, these fears trickle down to your kids, especially when you don't open your family up to opportunities.

Caution gives us pause before we jump headfirst into the unknown. It makes us do our research on a topic before we dive into it. Conversely, fear stops us from taking action even toward something that deep down we desperately want. Fear of failure keeps us from realizing dreams and leads to regret.

My big fear is that I am going to screw you up because of my own deficiencies. All I can do is try to do my best.

Now, I am not saying you shouldn't be afraid. You will and, at times, you should be. Sometimes there is a real reason to feel fear. As in all things, it is how you respond and react that matters. There are a few things, however, that I never want you to be afraid of, because there is no reason for it. Here they are: I never want you to be afraid of your mother or me. We will never put our hands on you no matter how angry we get. No matter what you have to say, we will always hear you out. Never be scared of saying anything to us (respectfully, of course).

I also don't want you to fear other people because you think they are better than you in some way. (In my eyes, there is no one *better* than you are, but we'll cover self-esteem at length throughout your life.) The real crime here would be to avoid trying something because your fear of being ostracized holds you back. Here is a gem for you, and you'll want to take this one with you wherever you go: You *will* be the subject of derision, laughter, hatred, jealousy, manipulation, cruelty, and indifference throughout your lifetime. How can I explain this, except to say that people are crazy sometimes? What I *can* promise is that if you aren't scared of these people or what they have to say, they won't hold you back. Is this easier said than done? Yes. Just try.

Before I delve into my examples of allowing fear to hold me back, I need to speak to you a moment about education. Can you guess that my examples have something to do with learning? Your mother and I have one hard and fast belief, and that is that your career from the age of five to twenty-five (and beyond) is your education. This doesn't mean you get out of housework, as we are all on that same team. What it does mean is that your goal, your vocation in life, should be to pursue your studies as best as you can. We'd like to expect straight A's, but all we can ask for is that you give it your best shot. You won't have to go it alone. We are here to help. Your quest will be a lifelong family project. We feel so strongly about this because we know that your ability to learn and retain that knowledge is the one thing that no one can take away from you. It is more important than wealth, power, or influence. Some might say that with an excellent education you could achieve all three of those things, but again, your mother and I would like you to be a kind, well-rounded, and educated person rather than an insufferable billionaire.

That being said, your mother and I share this

belief because we have been affected adversely by fear during our education, and we would like to help you navigate away from the same issues.

Parents are a child's first teachers. We have already talked about how important this role is. By letting their own fears cloud their child's mind, parents have already held their child back. Your mother and I will do everything we can not to let this happen.

The next teachers you will meet will be in preschool and beyond. Much to a controlling parent's chagrin, these teachers will have a huge influence on the child (just ask your mother about Mr. White in seventh grade). For parents who send their child to school every day, the huge fear is that this influence will be a negative one on their child. As parents we can make sure we are with you on your journey every step of the way, and hopefully pick schools that are a good fit for you in the first place. As I have said often, we must try our best always...parents and children.

So, here is the big confession. You will not have heard this before because I have not wanted to offer you an excuse in life or influence you in one way or another concerning this pastime, but here it is: I do not like to read.

Yeah. This one is bad, I know. If I do my

fatherhood job right, you will never know it until this page. The bottom line is that I do not comprehend well, so reading is a chore for me. An especially big, tiresome, aggravating chore, but I do it anyway. Want to know why? Well, one reason is because I have to, and another is because I should. It's good for me to read (and not just *Sports Illustrated*). Reading is a way we learn. But because of a snarky teacher and some even snarkier kids, I stopped trying until I met your mother. I always avoided reading aloud in class and I even took the ACT over the SAT because of my dislike of it. These were bad choices.

The absolute truth is that had I worked at reading comprehension, I would have gotten better. If a person has half a brain, he can get better at almost anything regarding schoolwork by practicing and working hard. As your mother will be glad to point out, I manage to comprehend sports stats that I read about just fine, so I must have at least half a brain that I could use to read something that will improve my mind.

During your entire childhood and beyond, you will see me read. I promise, because my fears of being laughed at or not understanding the first time around should not hold you back from being an excellent reader.

There is an ironic twist in all of this talk of education and fear that involves your mother and me and opposites attracting. Your mother is an excellent reader. I have pointed out that your mother is a brilliant woman. She is off-the-charts smart. However, because of difficulty with multiplication tables in the third grade and a highly insensitive pre-algebra teacher, your mother *fears* math, big time. It isn't because she can't do it. I have pointed out that she can do anything. She has what some might call a mental block about it. Guess what? You will never know it until you read this page. Our vow to you is that we will do our very best never to hold you back with our fears.

What links your mother's and my fears (along with those of so many other people) is that they involve anxiety about failing in front of an audience. This is a part of human nature. Fight against it. Remember what I said about opinions? It's vitally important that you don't allow these to hold you back from trying something over and over. You won't get better at anything unless you do. Your mother and I didn't like our first taste of defeat in math and reading so we shut down. I hope that will not be an option for you. Fear of failure is a stupid reason not to try something you might love. It's almost as bad as not doing something because somebody made fun of you for it. That is remarkably stupid. The lesson I hope to teach you is that you have nothing to fear but your reactions.

If you fear what others think of you, you aren't focusing enough on what is genuinely important—being the best you can be both on and off the course.

You can probably guess that my lesson on the course has to do with fear of failure. I have allowed what others think to unduly influence me so many times that there isn't enough ink in my printer to print them all out. I can tell you that I don't do it anymore. I can encourage you to play your own game.

An interesting note about kids, fear, and learning a sport comes from my experience as a teacher. Juniors are incredible to instruct—if their folks aren't advising them as well. The simple reason for this is that again, even in golf, parents project their own fears onto the child and often-times students develops a hiccup in their swing that never existed until their parents brought it up. Take for example the average over-the-water shot. Until a mom or dad says, "watch out for the water," most children aren't aware it's even there. They just want to swing the life out of the club, but now they are thinking too much. Now they are aware of the water and they are afraid of it. Guess what? Ninety-nine percent of the time they will hit the water on every shot.

After years of teaching, I am going to agree with Beami and say that kids are fearless. They never know to be self-conscious or paranoid or *afraid* of the outcome until someone points out they need to be, either by laughing at them or pointing out the pitfalls, or, even worse, yelling.

My experience with students is that the more strain you put them under (before they are ready for it) the worse the outcome. Now, I am sure Tiger Woods will argue with me, because the rumor is that his dad put lots of pressure on him while teaching him the game and it worked out for him. Whereas, yes, Tiger has a family, a yacht and celebrity status, I would argue that at the heart of it all he has nothing else but golf. It strikes me that he doesn't enjoy these other blessings very much. I can't pretend to have the first idea of what kind of a person Tiger Woods is, but I am making a judgment based on watching him for the last twelve years. I could be wrong, but my guess is that the burden of his fear of failure is all consuming and that there is no balance in his life.

Even now, golf seems to be failing Tiger which

is difficult for me to see as I have watched him from the beginning of his career and have been in awe of his immense talent. It was so hard for me to watch his fall from grace last year. It is a horrible thing to see people that seemingly have everything not realize joy in the simple beauties in life like a round of golf, their family or even a sunny day.

Numerous accounts exist in the sports world of a child snapping because of pressure or fear of failure foisted on them by their parents or contemporaries. Sometimes it takes thirty years for the kid to snap, but eventually it happens. Take Mary Pierce, Jennifer Capriati, and Andre Agassi in tennis; Jimmy Piersall in baseball and Sean O'Hair in golf as examples of what can happen when the fear of failure is introduced into the equation of sports coaching and parenting. I would think that would be enough evidence for you. Arguably, these athletes are some of the most successful in their sports, but at what cost?

These athletes are good examples (to me anyway) of how controlling parents can ruin the love of the game for a child. Once a fear of failure is instilled, it is hard to get rid of it. When taken to the extreme as in the case of these players, it seems inevitable that when their talent fails them, they suffer a mental breakdown. Mental strength in sports and life is so difficult to teach. In my opinion the parents of these contenders believed the only way to build a champion was to break them mentally.

I believe the exact opposite is true. It is imperative to praise a *child* for a job well done and not praise the inherent talent. What happens when the kid has an off day like every other human in the world? If the child knows that he worked as hard as he could that day then that is and should be enough. If he has a coach or parent whispering in his ear that he is letting his talent down he will come to believe that how well he performs is the sum total of his existence, his self-worth. With this mindset when he *wins*, it's a good day. When he *doesn't*, it's a horrible day.

Most especially disturbing to me is that parents who use pressure and fear to push their kids in sports try to justify their actions by saying the kid has a choice. Really? Because most armchair psychologists will tell you that all a kid wants is his parents' approval. So if your dad wants you to be the next Babe Ruth, you'll want it too, whether you like baseball or not. Call me Pollyanna, but I believe that if these kids are taught to love the sport first and to have *fun* no matter the outcome, then they will not only be successful at their game, but also as human beings.

Sean O'Hair is a wonder to me. His early years are a well-documented case of the coach-parent relationship morphing into something so negative I am surprised his father wasn't brought up on charges. In addition to the bizarre parenting skills of the dad, he also asked his *child* to sign a contract with him and claimed he was within his rights to collect money from his own son. Why Sean O'Hair is amazing to me is because somehow in all that negativity he realized what was important. He is firmly entrenched in golf. He is ranked in the top fifty players. He has had six professional wins since 1999. Quite impressive. What sincerely inspires me is that from the interviews I've read he seems like a balanced human being who "gets it." The man's mental game should be in ruins because of his early training. But in finding his wife and building a family with her, he found a balance. I believe he is a better player because of that balance. I can guarantee you that he is a better human for it.

Let me give you a clue here, Jax: Every person loses in sports and life. How you handle the loss is what makes you a champion.

So much talk in golf is focused on the mental

game. Why would any coach or parent think the best way to direct a kid on how to get into the zone is to teach him to question himself constantly? There is no possibility of true focus in life or sports if your mind is continually doing so. I am not saying not to practice. I am not saying don't give it everything you've got. If you're doing that then the brain game will follow.

Somewhere between knowing what to do (say, swing the club) and how to do it is a space in time that is totally controlled by your mind. It's that moment where self-doubt can creep in and make you question whether or not you *do* know what you are doing in either life or in golf. At this point you have to believe that the time you've put in, the practice, and the research will not fail you and you will be able to execute that which you so desire to accomplish.

As a teacher I can't control what is going on in my student's head. I can try to guide him and I can give him something positive to think about but even then, it is up to him to take the leap and believe in his abilities enough to execute the needed action.

At no other time in life or sports than during a crisis of confidence can the mind be so easily broken and so hard to fix. (Physical injuries are nothing compared to this mental blow.) That is something only faith will heal. If faith was easy to teach we'd all be believers.

Parents have a special responsibility to build that faith in a child's self. This is not just so the child can shoot par. This is something that pervades every aspect of a child's life. Whether he tries the slide at the playground or whether he sends in a resume for a job he really wants all depends on whether or not he believes in himself. I know some parents that are convinced it is their job to knock their kids "down a peg" or make sure they suffer setbacks so they learn from them. I pose this to them: Isn't the world hard enough without you celebrating the tribulations of your child and downplaying the triumphs? Bad stuff happens to people whether you want it to or not. The world will knock kids down a peg and they will suffer setbacks without a parent helping it along. In my opinion, we should be teaching kids how to get past this with their mental game intact. You don't accomplish this by teaching your child to expect that he deserved the bad stuff in the first place.

Jax, the inside game is a leap of faith at any time. Just make sure you surround yourself in life and sports with people who are willing to take the leap with you.

LESSON 9

Now would be a good time to talk about how to play the game. Safely? Conservatively? Aggressively? Without fear? A number of opinions exist on how to go about the game of golf. This simple conversation is about course management. "Should I hit a driver on each hole or should I play fairways and greens?" The answer lies within you and could vary from week to week, tournament to tournament, or even hole by hole. Tiger Woods is a great example of how to play the game. He very seldom contends in the events where the winner is twenty or more under par as his strength is making pars on the most difficult holes under the most demanding conditions (a truly outstanding talent).

There certainly is no reason to have fear, but there is reason to be smart. Some holes and shots will look good in your eyes and some won't. When they look favorable, you will have more confidence because you will have a much easier time visualizing the golf shot. However, the holes or shots that don't look good are the challenge. It is imperative that you hit **your** golf shot. Play the shot that you have the most confidence in; it doesn't matter if it is a tee shot that will cause you to hit less club off the tee and as many as four or five more clubs into the green. You have to know yourself, what shots you can hit and when to hit them. In tournament play, avoid the shots your mind is afraid of. Play the ones you know you have in your arsenal. Work on the problem areas during practice time to get *over your fear.*

Here is a quick example of what I'm talking about. Billy Casper won the US Open, and all four days he intentionally played short of the green on the same long par three. I believe he did this because he was playing to his strengths and avoiding the kind of shots that made him feel uncomfortable.

A second short example is in regards to a 435-yard par four at World Woods, where I hated the shape of the hole. I played it four times before I was smart enough not to hit a driver. The fifth time I hit a three-wood and made my first par on the hole. With a good drive (clearly I couldn't visualize that happening on this hole) I could hit an eight-iron into the green; instead I hit a three-wood off the tee and a four-iron into the green. My fear of being able to hit a driver held me back until I realized that I should be playing the hole my way instead of letting the hole play me.

Visualize it happening to prove to yourself that it can happen!

The End... Sort of

Jax, when thinking of how to close this book, I admittedly wanted to be profound and inspire you. In writing these lessons I wanted to explain how much golf and its teachings mean to me. I hope that I will be able to foster that love of the game in you. If you don't love golf as much as I do that is okay, too. I do hope you'll respect the game and the guidelines I have outlined here for you.

The golf lessons are important. How we play defines our character. Yes, we learn from our experiences of winning and losing, however the number on the scorecard means nothing to me if the player is not a gentlemen or a lady. Just like in life, how well we navigate the obstacles and challenges of those eighteen holes makes us the person we are.

Even more important are the life lessons we can learn from golf. The bunkers, tough terrain and hazards in the world beyond the course are even more difficult to manage, but you must figure out a way to handle them and still be able to sleep at night. I hope these teachings help you when playing your game and living your life.

If I haven't been profound, if I haven't inspired you so far, I won't manage it now. So, I figure I'll tell you a little about you at the age of two and make you a promise. I'll have to hope it's enough.

Most people will say I am biased when I speak of you. I am. You're my kid. I am also not the kind of person who sugarcoats things, so the two might balance out. If not, I don't care. You are my world. There is not a smaller way to describe what you are to me. Every decision I make is centered on you. This, in my opinion, is as it should be. If I was going to be a selfish bastard and not put you first, I shouldn't have had a kid in the first place. You didn't ask to be here. So there it is.

When you were born, you were beautiful. This isn't just a proud daddy talking. You were. Your looks seem to be heading in the direction of drop-dead gorgeous, or so I hear from nearly everyone else who meets you. You, your mom, and I are going to try our best to remember that while good looks are a nice perk, they are only due to the luck of the draw from the gene pool; there are so many more important things in life.

I will tell you some of the things I see in you that are important to me. You are smart. Unmistakably smart. If you weren't, I would still love you as much, but I won't lie and say I'm not happy that you seem to "get it." As far as milestones go, your mother assures me that you are off-the-charts advanced.

You are sweet. You are respectful. (Yes, I can see this even though you are only two.) You are curious and bright and you have a great sense of humor. You listen well and you have just the right amount of "go to hell" in you. Everything about you is a perfect combination.

These qualities still aren't what matter most to me. Even if none were true, I would still adore you just for being who you are. You have an endless capacity for love. You love me unconditionally. You, my best boy, try so hard. A father could ask for nothing more in a son. A son should always ask the same of his father. So my vow to you is this: I will never give up, and I will never say, "Do as I say, not as I do." I will always try. I will work to be the finest human being, manager, employee, husband and father I can be. I will be the best example I can be. You deserve the best.

The most important promise I can make to you is that I will love you, no matter what—even if you end up being a Yankees fan (and that, my son, is true love).

When I wrote this for you Jax, I had the idea that this book would be something I would want to give you when you turned eighteen or twenty-one. It's my hope that at that age, you will be ready for the life lessons I outlined here. As far as the golf lessons here go, I hope that I have taught them all to you by the time you get to that age and that you can use these for reference when needed.

Mostly though, I wrote this for you because at some point you will go out into this world without me, a journey that can be overwhelmingly diffi-cult at times, and you will feel alone. This book is just a simple reminder that no matter where you are, I'll always be there if you need me.

As you go out into the world, my heart breaks open and sends you forth with all my love.

Love,
Daddy

About the Author

Tim Beckwith is a PGA Master Professional in Instruction, an honor afforded only a small group of golf professionals. He serves as director of golf at The Oaks Club in Osprey, Florida.

photo by Rebecca DeAngelo

Bob Thomas
Author of *Ben Hogan's Secret*

Keep tapping into your love for the game! Your life as well as your golf game will continue to improve. Love automatically improves our lives. All we have to do is use it – and golf is the game that lets us do that. It gives us something to love.

Yours in golf,

Bob Thomas

With golf eBooks, you can play your mental game –
and improve
Go to:

ebooksforgolfers.com